# CONTENTS

| | | |
|---|---|---|
| Acronyms and Abbreviations | | 2 |
| Acknowledgements | | 2 |
| Introduction | | 2 |
| 1 | Turkey Before the Second World War | 5 |
| 2 | The Turkish Armed Forces | 8 |
| 3 | Threats and Opportunities | 19 |
| 4 | Salonika Front | 22 |
| 5 | The Balkans and the Soviet Union 1940–1941 | 26 |
| 6 | Encirclement 1941–1942 | 39 |
| 7 | Diplomacy and Deception 1943–1944 | 47 |
| 8 | Endgame | 64 |
| 9 | Conclusion | 73 |
| Appendices | | |
| I | Main Characters | 75 |
| II | Chronology | 76 |
| Bibliography | | 77 |
| Notes | | 80 |
| About the Author | | 84 |

Helion & Company Limited
Unit 8 Amherst Business Centre
Budbrooke Road
Warwick
CV34 5WE
England
Tel. 01926 499 619
Email: info@helion.co.uk
Website: www.helion.co.uk
Twitter: @helionbooks
Visit our blog http://blog.helion.co.uk/

Text © Dave Watson 2023
Photographs © as individually credited
Colour artwork © David Bocquelet, Renato Dalmaso, Peter Penev and Goran Sudar 2023
Maps drawn by and © Dave Watson 2023 unless otherwise credited

Designed and typeset by Farr out Publications, Wokingham, Berkshire
Cover design Paul Hewitt, Battlefield Design (www.battlefield-design.co.uk)

Every reasonable effort has been made to trace copyright holders and to obtain their permission for the use of copyright material. The author and publisher apologise for any errors or omissions in this work, and would be grateful if notified of any corrections that should be incorporated in future reprints or editions of this book.

ISBN 978-1-804510-26-1

British Library Cataloguing-in-Publication Data
A catalogue record for this book is available from the British Library

All rights reserved. No part of this publication may be reproduced, stored in a retrieval system, or transmitted, in any form, or by any means, electronic, mechanical, photocopying, recording or otherwise, without the express written consent of Helion & Company Limited.

We always welcome receiving book proposals from prospective authors.

Note: In order to simplify the use of this book, all names, locations and geographic designations are as provided in *The Times World Atlas*, or other traditionally accepted major sources of reference, as of the time of described events.

# ACRONYMS AND ABBREVIATIONS

| | | | |
|---|---|---|---|
| **EDES** | National Democratic Greek League | **OKH** | Oberkommando des Heeres – German Upper Command of the Army |
| **ELAS** | Military wing of the communist dominated Greek National Liberation Front | **OKW** | Oberkommando der Wehrmacht – German Armed Forces High Command |
| **LSF** | Levant Schooner Flotilla | **PZL** | Państwowe Zakłady Lotnicze – Polish State Aviation Works |
| **MEH or MAH** | Milli Emniyet Hizmeti – Turkish National Security Service | **RAF** | Royal Air Force (British) |
| **MTB** | Motor Torpedo Boat | **SIME** | Security Intelligence Middle East |
| **NCO** | Non-Commissioned Officer | **SOE** | Special Operations Executive |
| **NKGB** | Soviet Union, People's Commissariat for State Security | **Stavka** | High command of the Soviet armed forces |
| | | **TDA** | Turkish Diplomatic Archives |
| **NKVD** | Soviet Union, People's Commissariat for Internal Affairs | **VKJ** | Vojska Kraljevine Jugoslavije – Royal Yugoslav Army |

# ACKNOWLEDGEMENTS

I am grateful to the historians who inspired my interest in the history of the Balkans and who have contributed to my understanding of Turkey during this period. In particular, Frank Weber, Selim Deringil, Nicholas Tamkin, Robin Denniston and Edward Weisband. This includes the work of Elizabeth Barker and Christopher Catherwood, which cover Turkey in the broader context of the region. I am also indebted to the people of the Balkans who have been so welcoming during my many visits, also to my wife and our daughter for their forbearance during these 'holidays'. To these, I would add fellow enthusiasts who have contributed ideas and content through the website *Balkan Military History* (www.balkanhistory.org) during the 23 years I have been its editor.

My thanks to all those institutions and their staff who assisted with the research for this book, including but not limited to: The National Archives Kew, The British Library, The Mitchell Library Glasgow, The National Library of Scotland and many museums in the countries that make up the Balkans today.

Whilst there are surprisingly few accessible primary Turkish sources, I am grateful to my friends in modern Türkiye for pointing me in the right direction, although any errors and opinions are my own. I have generally followed the modern spelling of place names and other words. For example, British documents of the period and even the Foreign Office, who should have known better, persisted in using the old name of the Turkish capital, Angora, instead of Ankara. Surnames can confuse non-Turkish readers because they were only adopted in 1935. So, Mustafa Kemal takes the surname Atatürk (Father of the Nation) and Ismet takes İnönü after the battle he won in 1921.

Getting Turkey into the Second World War and attacking the 'soft underbelly' of Europe was an almost exclusively British project, with military support from across the Empire. The Soviets blew hot and cold on the project; the Americans were sceptical and at best went along with the British position. Even amongst the British leadership there was considerable scepticism, which left Churchill as the most consistent advocate of the project throughout the war. For this reason, British primary sources provide an important part of this book.

# INTRODUCTION

In 1888, Otto von Bismarck famously said, 'The whole of the Balkans is not worth the bones of a single Pomeranian grenadier'. Notwithstanding that great statesman's view, the Balkans has played an important role throughout history as the link between two continents.[1] Nowhere is that link more evident than at the Straits and its narrowest points in the Bosporus and the Dardanelles in the modern state of Turkey.

Studies of the Second World War traditionally begin with the rise of Hitler and the failure of the western democracies to challenge fascism in the Spanish Civil War and through their appeasement policies. Important though these events were, Turkey and the Balkans played a crucial role at key moments during the conflict. Unlike his generals, who generally shared Bismarck's view, Hitler understood Germany's need for the natural resources of the Balkans, including Turkish chromite and Romanian oil. As an Austrian, he also remembered the events of 1918. Turkey was similarly important to Stalin, who saw the Straits as a route into the Black Sea and the Soviet Union. His view of Russia's security was based more on the Tsarist world view than Lenin's revolutionary vision. Churchill was another of the key players in our story whose interest in Turkey went back to the Gallipoli campaign of the First World War. An interest, some might say an obsession, which he maintained during the interwar years and throughout the Second World War. The 'soft underbelly' was Churchill's shorthand for attacking Germany through Turkey and the Balkans. Whilst Turkey

Winston Churchill. (United Nations)

is typically a footnote in most histories of the Second World War, it featured highly in the strategies of the combatants.

Turkey's neutrality in the Second World War until 1945, has been described as a balance struck between the conflicting tugs of interventionism and noninterventionism – with the latter winning. Allied frustration grew during the war, particularly after the tide turned in late 1942 following the victories at El Alamein and Stalingrad. What is often forgotten is Turkey's concern about Soviet Union expansionism, which they believed the Allies underestimated. This was also a factor in the foreign policy of Balkan countries that joined the Axis. As the war drew to a conclusion, they feared that the British and Americans would negotiate a sphere of influence agreement that placed Turkey in the Soviet orbit. It is possible to get an understanding for this view by looking at the map orientation of Turkish military studies of the campaigns. If, like them, the observer turns the map around and looks at Europe from Turkey's angle, it gives a very different perspective.

It is now known from the Soviet archives, that the Nazi-Soviet Pact was not a comprehensive agreement over the Balkans. However, Turkey and the Balkan states did not know that in 1940. As Catherwood argues,[2] alienating Hitler was risky enough but to alienate Stalin as well, would be very dangerous. This led Romania and Bulgaria to join the Axis whilst Yugoslavia and Greece were invaded and occupied. Turkey, therefore, sought to initially protect itself from the sandwich of German expansion in the Balkans and their pact partner, the Soviet Union, until June 1941. After that, they sought Great Power protection, primarily from the threat of the Soviet Union, as the Ottoman Empire had done from Russia throughout the nineteenth century. It has been argued that the Allies never really understood this,[3] and negotiations failed to reach the level of candour required.

Britain was the main allied nation to focus on Turkey during the war. This is traditionally viewed as part of Churchill's 'soft underbelly' approach to defeating Germany or his desire to protect the Empire. A.J.P. Taylor called this approach a 'will o' the wisp'.[4] Modern studies question this view and point to a wider range of opinions in wartime Britain and even before Churchill came to power. Churchill also understood that for Britain to win the war, it needed allies. The USA

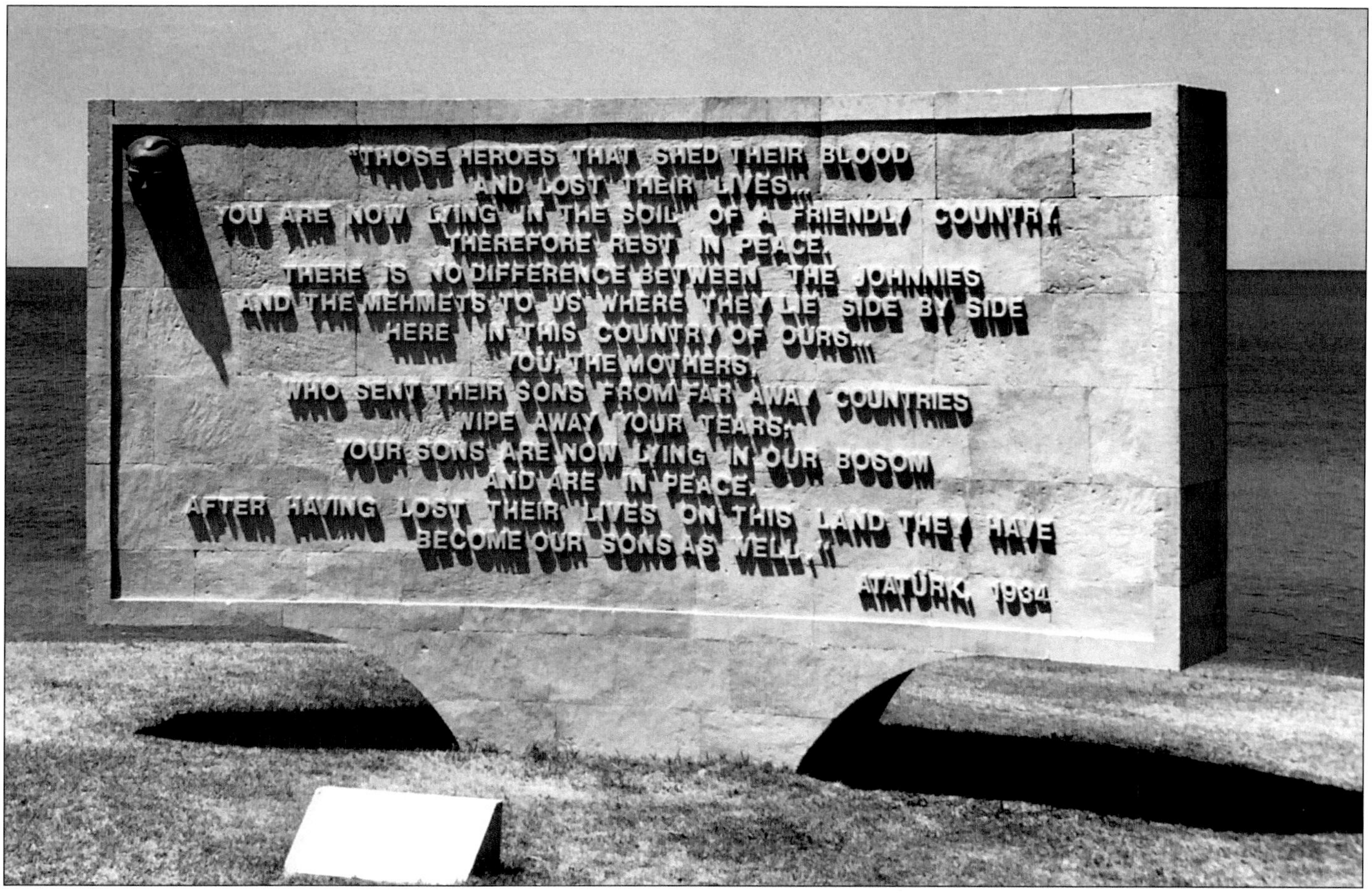

Gallipoli memorial that reflects positive relations between Britain and Turkey before the Second World War. It is doubtful that Atatürk used these actual words. (Photo by Author)

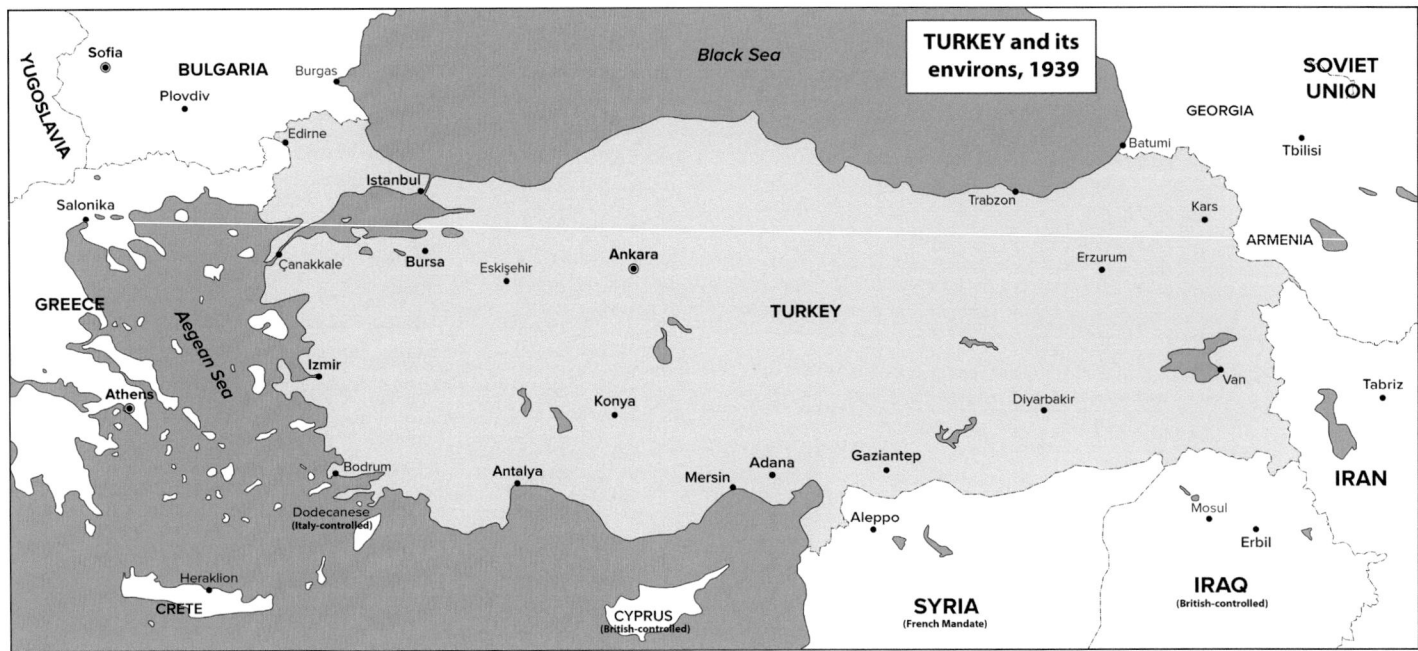

Turkey and Its Environs in 1939. (Author)

and USSR eventually delivered but in 1940 they were not available, so Churchill had to look elsewhere. However, even much later in the war, Churchill persisted in his Turkish project despite being advised that their military usefulness to the Allies was marginal.

Churchill, whatever impression the Gallipoli campaign may give, was not opposed to Turkey. Despite his wartime use of Christian rhetoric and avowedly Christian nationalism, he was anything but dogmatic on religion.[5] He also accepted the martial races theory and admired the fighting qualities of Muslim troops. He had visited Istanbul before the First World War and corresponded with the Young Turk leadership. After the war, he urged a 'good peace', mainly as a bulwark against his real concern, the Bolsheviks.

By 1940, Churchill believed that Turkey was the most powerful neutral, which due to its strategic position, could influence the outcome of the war. He also had the benefit of access to the Turkish military and diplomatic cyphers, something he had made use of during and after the First World War and returned to in 1940.[6] He used these to assess Turkish plans to stay neutral during the Second World War. They also encouraged him to regularly return to his Balkan offensive concept, launched from Turkey up to the Danube and on into the German heartland. Most of his military and foreign policy advisers were less enthusiastic and the Americans were distinctly unenthusiastic.

It is certainly the case that Britain had a favourable view of modern Turkey and viewed it as the key to the Balkans. It was also seen as a bridge to relations with the Soviet Union, at least in the early war period. There may have been an overestimation of Turkish military capabilities early in the war, which only shifted due to Turkish rebuffs and closer military inspection. For example, there were 128 staff meetings between the British and Turkish military between November 1942 and November 1943. During the war, Churchill often referenced the impact the collapse of Bulgaria had on the Central Powers in the First World War.

Surprisingly, little has been written in Turkey on the military aspects of the period and even the published list in the military archives have a gap between 1938 and 1950. Even the excellent Istanbul Military Museum has a large gap in its exhibition rooms between the end of the War of Independence and the Korean War. The Turkish General Staff published the memoirs of Turkish officers during the war,[7] which is an honest appraisal of the armed forces limited preparedness to fight a modern war. The standard history argues that Turkey sought a non-belligerent approach,[8] seeking freedom of movement and avoiding alignment with power blocs, 'Peace at home and peace abroad' was the slogan. Although Atatürk qualified this by stressing the importance of the country's capability to protect against aggression – peace was contingent on preparedness for war – Turkey sought a defensive posture in which pragmatism triumphed over promises, idealism and certainly ideology. We should not forget that Turkish leaders had fought in several wars and understood the impact on their country. On his death bed in 1938, Mustafa Kemal advised, 'A world war is near. In the course of this war, international equilibrium will be entirely destroyed. If during this period we act unwisely and make the smallest mistake, we will be faced with an even graver catastrophe than in the armistice years'.

The world may have been engaged in a titanic struggle but the Turkish leadership cannot be blamed for insulating their people. Even if, for a country at a pivotal world crossroads, that would be a challenge. This is the story of how the Turkish leadership managed to keep Turkey out of the war until 1945 and the many plans to engage them as the war raged around their country.

# 1
# TURKEY BEFORE THE SECOND WORLD WAR

On 3 March 1924, the Turkish Grand National Assembly abolished the Caliphate. The next day, Sultan Abdulmecit left Istanbul, ending 640 years of the Ottoman dynasty.

The Turkish Republic was the beginning of a new era of Turkish history. The Treaty of Lausanne, signed on 24 July 1923, secured the borders of the new state and removed the foreign rights and privileges forced on Turkey after its defeat in the First World War. The last British troops left Istanbul on 2 October 1923. On 29 October, the Grand National Assembly voted for a new constitution that declared Turkey to be a republic, with Mustapha Kemal Atatürk as the first president and Ismet İnönü the first prime minister.

The Turks had won their independence after the Greek-Turkish War of 1919–1922, usually known in Turkey as the War of Independence. In May 1919, the victorious wartime allies encouraged (and financed) the Greeks to invade western Anatolia, an area that had a significant Greek population. Not that the Greek premier, Venizelos, needed much encouragement as the invasion allowed him to pursue the *Megali Idea* (Great Idea), a Greek state that would include the large Greek populations within the Ottoman Empire. After an initial advance from the port of Smyrna (Izmir), the Greek army overstretched itself with an advance on Ankara. This advance was held by the new Turkish Nationalist Army led by General Mustapha Kemal (Atatürk), initially by Ismet İnönü (the future President) at what became known as the first and second battles of İnönü. The Turkish Great Summer Offensive in 1922, resulted in a complete victory for the Turks.[1]

The war was accompanied by widespread atrocities against civilians by both sides, coupled with ethnic cleansing. This culminated in the internationally recognised relocation of 1.7 million people in 1922–1923, Greeks from Anatolia and Muslims from Greece. This ethnic cleansing on a massive scale, created a smaller, predominately ethnic Turkish state. These population transfers resulted in peoples who did not speak Turkish and, vice versa, being moved to a country that they had no links with. For example, the Turkish speaking Orthodox Karamanlis were expelled to a country they had no affiliation with and did not speak the language. The test, unusually for a secular, nation-building project, was effectively, religion, not language, with Kemal even using the 'nation of Islam' rhetoric during the war.[2] Ethnic cleansing was not a new concept, with some two million Muslims leaving the Balkans by the end of the nineteenth century and smaller numbers of Greeks and Bulgarians, going in the other direction. Domestic enemies, such as the Kurds, were also suppressed to silence opposition to the national struggle and minorities were generally regarded as destabilising factors.

The Turks had won their independence but a decade of war had decimated the population and wrecked the economy. Some 2.5 million Turks died during the wars, leaving a population of just over 13 million in the new state. The dismantling of the Ottoman bureaucracy stabilised government spending but foreign trade was drastically curtailed and inflation rocketed.

Mustafa Kemal used his military reputation to build a very different Turkey. His ideology became known as Kemalism based on Republicanism, Nationalism, Popularism and Revolutionism, delivered through Secularism and Statism. The historiography was

Mustafa Kemal (Atatürk). (Public Domain)

set out in a six-day speech (Nutuk) to the Republican People's Party in October 1927. This was not a western democracy but neither did it adopt many of the extreme forms of nationalism seen later in Italy and Germany. Kemal described Hitler as a 'tin-peddler' and was horrified at the language and thoughts in *Mein Kampf*,[3] and he was similarly dismissive of Mussolini's Italy. However, he respected Stalin, predicting his longevity if nothing else. This, together with the traditional Turkish wariness of Russia, made him very careful in his diplomatic dealings with the Soviet Union. He aimed to unify the Turkish people around common goals, creating a modern state. It was also based on a status quo foreign policy, which did not chase great ideas or 'fantasies', returning Turkey to 'our natural, legitimate limits'.

The new Republic introduced extensive social, cultural and economic changes. The most radical was the abolition of the Caliphate, removing religion from the political realm. The emancipation of women, a new alphabet, land reform, economic plans and even a new interpretation of the history of the Turks were driven forward by Kemal. The changes were introduced at a remarkable pace and were resisted by some both politically and militarily. They were not without their problems, particularly for Istanbul. Charles King's book, *Midnight at the Pera Palace*,[4] describes the changes as the capital was moved to Ankara. Dress regulations changed and even the calendar and clocks were brought into line with Europe. Political life was closed down but the brothels, bars and clubs continued, albeit under Turkish ownership.

Turkish nationalism was not hostile to its neighbours. In 1926, it signed a treaty with Great Britain surrendering rights to Mosul in return for 10 percent of the oil produced. They even signed a treaty of friendship with Greece in October 1930, which included a clause on naval equality in the eastern Mediterranean. This was followed by a raft of treaties with European states and Turkey joined the League of Nations in July 1932. In 1934, Turkey joined

Turkish soldiers and local people in the Dersim region. (Turkish Army, Public Domain)

the Balkan Entente Treaty with Greece, Yugoslavia and Romania, which guaranteed each other's territorial integrity, primarily against aggression from another Balkan state. However, there was a secret protocol providing for mutual assistance if attacked by a non-Balkan power if a Balkan state joined the aggression. However, Turkey and Greece declared that the Entente was not to involve them in a war with any Great Power, which somewhat diluted the effect of the protocol. The obvious non-signatory and the main target of the Entente was Bulgaria, which had territorial ambitions in Thrace and elsewhere. In 1936, an agreement was reached with the signatories to the Lausanne treaty allowing Turkey to resume sovereignty of the Straits (Montreux Convention). A long-standing dispute with France over the Syrian province of Alexandretta (Hatay) was only resolved as part of a non-aggression pact in 1939, even though the area did not have a Turkish majority. A deal was 'encouraged' by Atatürk personally moving troops to the border and this followed Turkish support for the Alawis in Syria as a way of putting additional pressure on the French.[5] The Saadabad Pact of 1937 with Iraq, Iran and Afghanistan secured the eastern borders.

The new state faced some early revolts. The Kurds in south-eastern Anatolia, who constituted around 20 percent of the population of Turkey, revolted several times between 1925 and 1929 and again in 1937–1939 during the infamous Dersim rebellion or massacre.[6] The military leadership of Marshall Çakmak took harsh and humiliating measures to suppress any threat of rebellion, which included burning villages and massacring the inhabitants. He even clamped down on education, arguing that this would make the Kurds less likely to rebel.[7] Deportations followed this to Thrace and Western Turkey, a policy that started in 1916 and went through several stages into the 1930s with a focus on deporting religious, intellectual and social elites.[8] The Treaty of Sevres (1920) set out a procedure for establishing a Kurdish state, encompassing many Kurds spread across Turkey and Iraq, if not Iran and Syria.[9] However, that provision did not survive the Treaty of Lausanne (1923). The British played along with autonomy in neighbouring Iraq before dropping the idea when Iraq was granted nominal independence in 1930.

Ismet İnönü. (Official Photo. Public Domain)

The aim of creating a solely Turkish state was nuanced by calling the Kurds 'mountain Turks' and legislation sought to eliminate their language and culture – even the word 'Kurd' was declared illegal. However, the ethnic nature of any state is a complex process developing over time. The same is true of the population of Anatolia, which assimilated in a series of migrations, aided by the Ottomans who subsumed populations rather than destroying them. Atatürk himself did not adopt an ethnic nationalism, he took the view that the people of Turkey together made up the nation and İnönü included the Kurds in his definition of the 'Muslim majorities' of the National Pact.[10] Nevertheless, military action in particular, created further Kurdish reaction that continues to the present day. The weakness of the Kurds has always been the internal division between tribes, language dialects, religious practice and the different states they have resided in. They have been divided by those governments and other outside powers but have also divided themselves, rarely coming together with a common political goal.

Political opposition from conservative elements and others, gained support at different times. Whilst the state was secular, including the education system, it remained a Muslim society, although religious leaders lost their influence. By 1930, Turkey had effectively become a one-party state, although arguably with less oppression than in other dictatorships of the period. Not that opposition leaders hanged for treason would agree. Democratic reforms were attempted but usually collapsed as the leadership deemed the country was not ready for such freedoms. That does not mean there was no political opposition. Christine Philliou explains the Turkish notion of political opposition and dissent known as *muhalefet*, to weave together the Ottoman and Turkish periods.[11]

There were agricultural reforms to improve food production but industrialisation was slow. By the 1930s, Turkey turned to increased state control with two Five-Year Plans on the Soviet model. These modestly increased production and resulted in a trade surplus for most of the 1930s. State budgets largely balanced and the value of the Turkish *Lira* increased on world markets. Military expenditure now took no more than 30 percent of the budget.

Mustafa Kemal Atatürk died on 10 November 1938 and was succeeded by Ismet İnönü. A veteran of the First World War, İnönü recognised the damage Turkish involvement in the conflict had done to the state. Turkish foreign policy was openly based on peace, friendship and trade with all nations and had few territorial aims. Internally, İnönü had absolute control over the Assembly. New political parties were banned, the press was strictly controlled and trade unions were banned. The political model was closer to Italy and Germany than the western democracies. However, the four main issues facing Turkey remained throughout the period – developing the state, expanding or limiting the bureaucracy and the military, defining the nation and establishing good relations with the main powers.[12] While his policies were viewed as an extension of Atatürk's, he brought back into the fold some of the old opposition who had opposed Atatürk's increasing personal power.

Turkey was involved in several international alliances. King Edward VIII visited Istanbul in 1936 and İnönü attended the coronation of George VI in 1937. Britain also provided credit for the second Five-Year Plan. On 19 October 1939, Turkey entered into a mutual assistance agreement with Britain and France, which included loans to help Turkey re-arm. It did not require Turkey to participate in a war unless they were threatened. Many in the British government, particularly the Treasury, argued that the agreement was lopsided but it reflected the Foreign Office's view that Britain needed Turkey's support in the Mediterranean. Turkey already had obligations to support Romania and Greece under the terms of the earlier Balkan Pact and Turkey was very concerned over the Nazi-Soviet alliance of August 1939. Russia threatened Turkey to keep the Allies out of the Balkans and sought an agreement to close the Straits to foreign warships with a garrison of Russian troops. The Turkish foreign minister even suggested to Britain in October 1938 that Turkish troops garrison Egypt.[13] A proposal not well received by the Foreign Office, who viewed it as an attempt to restore Turkish jurisdiction over Egypt. Turkey revived this proposal several times during the Second World War.

Britain was keen to keep Turkey engaged because of its commitments in the Balkans. The Foreign Office gave Anglo-Turkish relations a high priority in the 1930s because they saw Turkey as protecting British trade routes and oil interests in the Middle East. They also viewed Turkey as a bridge between Britain and the Soviet Union, if only because the Turks were prepared to engage with the Soviet Union. Even so, diplomatic reports show that the embassy had little understanding of the country outside the cities and embassy staff rarely ventured out into the interior.[14] Britain's commitment to Poland is well known but less familiar, is the similar promises given to Greece and Romania. Announcing the guarantees, Chamberlain said, 'His Majesty's Government attach the greatest importance to the avoidance of disturbance by force or threats of force of the status quo in the Mediterranean and the Balkan Peninsula'. Greece was at least linked to Britain's traditional maritime polices but intervention in Romania needed Turkish or Soviet support. The latter was a non-starter after the Nazi-Soviet Pact and Turkey was wary of such a policy. British public opinion was generally positive towards modern Turkey compared to the previous Ottoman 'sick man of Europe' rhetoric.

Maintaining the status quo in the Balkans gave Germany an advantage over Britain. Hitler had no such qualms over territorial revisionism and could offer incentives to countries like Hungary, which wanted Transylvania back from Romania and the Dobruja region of Romania to Bulgaria. The Balkans were littered with similar claims. Germany also made its own efforts to bring Turkey into the Axis and they were the major supplier of iron and steel, machinery and chemicals to Turkey. In return, Germany received half of all Turkish exports, including 70 percent of cotton and chromite. Franz von Papen, who had served in Turkey during the First World War, was sent to Ankara as the new German ambassador.

Franz von Papen. (Bundesarchiv, Bild 183-1988-0113-500 / CC-BY-SA 3.0, CC BY-SA 3.0)

Turkey had signed a 150 million marks credit agreement in July 1938 and the Turkish Foreign Office indicated privately to Ribbentrop that they would block support to Poland through the Straits.[15] Germany was prepared to buy Turkish tobacco, an important export. Whereas the British government decided it was useless to try and change the tastes of the British smoker. Turco-German trade was worth around 280 million marks annually by the end of 1938, which constituted 44 percent of exports and 48 percent of imports. In contrast, British figures were 3 percent for exports and 11 percent for imports. The most important export was chromite, used for high-grade steel, with Germany importing one-third of their requirements from Turkey.

Cultural and propaganda links with Germany were developed. There was a daily German-language newspaper, the *Türkische Post* and other newspapers publicised Nazi perspectives along with radio programmes and sponsored lectures. This was taken up in the largest circulation Turkish paper *Cumhuriyet* (The Republic), whose owner was sympathetic to Germany. The paper was briefly closed down after urging Turkey to join the war on Germany's side in July 1940. The consistent propaganda line was that Germany could offer Turkey protection against Soviet expansionism. Less attractive to the Nazis was Turkey's pragmatic policy of sheltering Jewish experts, dismissed by them in the 1930s. Thousands of professors, physician's, artists, laboratory workers and others were welcomed into Turkey and given jobs, including in Istanbul and Ankara universities. The authorities also closed down anti-Semitic newspapers in the 1930s.[16]

Papen's diplomatic aims were to make Turkey part of an axis of encirclement. He claimed İnönü was sympathetic to Hitler but concerned about Mussolini's occupation of Albania. Attempts by the Italians to reassure the Turks that Albania was not a jumping-off point for further territorial aggrandisement, did not reassure the Turks. They remembered that in the 1930s, Italian schools taught that Anatolia should be part of a new Italian Empire as it had been in Roman times. Papen even went as far as suggesting that Italy abandon some of the Dodecanese islands. Turkey's diplomatic relations with Italy were not always hostile.[17] Mussolini's diplomacy was fluid and inconsistent, leading to periods of rapprochement with Turkey, even supplying ships for the Turkish Navy.

The German General Staff considered the merits of a Turkish alliance. They doubled the number of technical instructors in the Turkish army and their military attaché, Colonel Rohde, prepared a favourable report. He argued that Turks could create havoc with Britain's land bridge to India through the Middle East, threatening the Suez Canal and oil supplies from Persia. The Germans calculated that the Soviet Union was too weak to intervene and Mussolini conceded that he did not have the resources to make good on his claims in the eastern Mediterranean. However, a botched arms deal with Saudi Arabia resulted in the Turks pulling out. This was part of a broader German plan to support revolts against the British in the Islamic world. During the war, Hitler put the Mufti of Jerusalem on the payroll to the tune of 75,000 marks a month, together with a luxury house in Berlin.[18] Amongst a range of plots, the Mufti helped raise Muslim units in Bosnia, including the *Handschar* SS Division. As an aside, one of the Mufti's fellow plotters was Saddam Hussein's uncle.

*Handschar* SS troops. (Bundesarchiv, Bild 101III-Mielke-036-23 / Mielke / CC-BY-SA 3.0, CC BY-SA 3.0 DE)

Turkey's relations with the Soviet Union during the interwar period had been reasonably positive. There were tensions among non-Turkish ethnic groups on the border, which the Soviets occasionally stirred up. On the other hand, Mustafa Kemal adopted some Soviet practices and economic links had been encouraged. In September 1939, the Turkish foreign minister went to Moscow with the prospect of a Turkish-Soviet Pact. Stalin used this as bait to persuade Turkey to water down their agreement with Britain and France. The talks broke down over Soviet demands to close the Straits to non-Black Sea powers and the Soviets largely blamed the British for the collapse. However, a protocol in the treaty with Britain exempted Turkey from any operation against the Soviet Union. The Soviets had their own territorial targets in the Balkans. Ribbentrop had given the all-clear in 1939 for the Soviets to annex Bessarabia but the Soviets went further and added Bukovina.

Turkey's main concern in the run-up to the war was Bulgaria. Turkey wanted a larger border area in Thrace to protect Edirne and stationed most of its best army units on that border. As part of its efforts to bring Bulgaria into the Balkan bloc, the British encouraged better relations, including a series of visits in late 1939 and early 1940 by Turkish Foreign Office officials. However, it was the Nazi-Soviet Pact that most worried the Turks. Papen did his best to minimise the impact but to Turkey, it opened the prospect of being surrounded by potentially hostile powers.

With hindsight, we can view the actions of Turkey in the pre-war period as a largely straightforward application of their policy objectives. However, in 1939, the position in the Balkans and the Middle East were much more complex and as we will see, a wide range of outcomes were possible.

# 2

# THE TURKISH ARMED FORCES

The new republic, once international treaties had established its borders, had other spending priorities than the armed forces. Consequently, Turkey's armed forces were not in a strong position at the outbreak of the Second World War.

Atatürk was reconciled to the loss of the Arab provinces. While he recognised the dangers to peacetime trade and wartime defences of foreign control of the Aegean islands, his focus after clearing the Greeks from Anatolia was to build up Turkey internally. İnönü was open to opportunities to gaining territory in a period when Hitler and Mussolini were redrawing the boundaries of Europe. However, he knew the Turkish army, which was only 200,000 strong, with few modern weapons, was an unlikely tool for foreign aggrandisement.

At İnönü's direction, readiness was tested with manoeuvres in Thrace during the summer of 1939. The army defended against an

# CHASING THE SOFT UNDERBELLY: TURKEY AND THE SECOND WORLD WAR

British propaganda article on the Turkish armed forces. (*War Illustrated*, 11 November 1939)

## TURKISH ARMY

### Organisation

The Army was organised into 11 army corps, grouped into three army inspectorates-general on a territorial basis, which would form the basis for army commands in wartime. The exception was eastern Thrace, which due to a small population, was supplemented by recruits from elsewhere in the country. Fortress commands mainly operated independently of territorial corps, manning often extensive fortifications in Thrace, Gallipoli, Istanbul, Izmir and Erzerum (facing the Soviet Union in the Caucasus).

The army in peacetime consisted of:

- 24 infantry divisions
- Three cavalry divisions
- One guard regiment
- Three mountain brigades
- One armoured brigade
- Seven fortress groups
- 11 frontier guard regiments
- Nine customs battalions and five independent companies
- 11 mobile gendarmerie regiments (subordinate to the Ministry of the Interior)

The mobile army was concentrated in Thrace, Western Anatolia and on the border with the Soviet Union.

Under the military law of 1927,[3] all males between the age of 20 to 41 were subject to conscription. The peacetime army took 80,000 recruits each year by conscription, although different classes could be called up in different parts of the country, that were aged 21, 22 or 23. They served on active duty for three years and then remained in reserve until age 41. This resulted in an army of between 130,000 and 170,000 in the summer, reducing to half that number in winter. Those selected disproportionately came from rural areas, making up 90 percent of the manpower when only 75 percent lived in these areas. In wartime, the plan was to mobilise an additional 16 infantry divisions.

An army corps would typically have an HQ of a cavalry squadron and infantry company. It included a medium artillery regiment of 36 guns of 155mm and 120mm and at least some anti-aircraft artillery and army cooperation aircraft. In addition, there would be specialist troops, including signals and engineer battalions, along with a field hospital and veterinary services. The main fighting arm consisted of

attack from Bulgaria and civil defence drills were held in Istanbul. This was repeated in 1940 with an RAF officer assisting and drafting a lessons learned report.[1] Despite the public show of approval, the exercises convinced İnönü that the Turkish military was not prepared for war. Military expenditure increased from 30 percent of the total government budget in 1938 to 53 percent in 1943, with a consequential impact on the domestic economy.

British propaganda at the time took a much more positive spin on the state of the Turkish army. The wartime broadsheet *War Illustrated* published an article in November 1939 under the heading 'The Guardians of the Straits are Ready Now'.[2] This includes pictures of Turkish ships and army equipment with the caption, 'The Turkish Army is now one of the most formidable fighting machines in the Mediterranean zone'.

German supplied 37mm anti-tank gun. (Author)

Russian supplied BA-6 armoured car. (Author, Central Armed Forces Museum Moscow)

two infantry divisions in peacetime, increasing to three in wartime with other formations like mountain brigades attached as required. This resulted in an army corps of around 39,000 men and 144 guns.

An infantry division would have similar specialist units, although at company strength, with supply and bakery detachments. In wartime, there would be three infantry regiments totalling 7,839 men and 246 officers, supported by 108 machine-guns. Each regiment had close-support guns, which were being replaced by nine anti-tank guns per regiment. The division would have two artillery regiments in wartime with 36 guns. Typically, two battalions of two batteries of four 75mm field guns and one battery of four 105mm howitzers. Plus, one battalion of three 105mm pack howitzer batteries.

Infantry regiments had three battalions. Battalions consisted of three rifle companies and a medium machine-gun company of 12 guns. A company had three platoons with three battle-groups of 14 men including an LMG and French Lebel grenade throwers. Each regiment had a platoon of three 81mm mortars, with plans to expand it to a three-platoon company. Regiment colours were intended to be carried in a war for morale purposes.

The three cavalry divisions (numbered 1, 2 and 14) each had three sabre regiments and one lancer regiment, supported by 36 machine guns and 24 field guns. They were typically brigaded in pairs, although this was not a permanent organisational feature. A cavalry regiment consisted of four sabre and one machine gun squadron. A squadron had 105 men organised into three troops.

Mountain brigades consisted of two mountain infantry regiments and a mountain artillery battalion. The 18th was based at Mugla (SW Turkey), 39th at Islahie (Syrian border) and the Agri mountain brigade (Mount Ararat). A mountain regiment had three battalions organised as infantry battalions.

There were coastal defence brigades at Izmir and Izmit with a mix of infantry and artillery units. Anti-aircraft defence units were mainly allotted to fortresses and ports.

The single armoured brigade had a motorised infantry regiment of two battalions and a motorcycle battalion, plus a tank battalion and an armoured car battalion. This was based in Thrace (Luleburgaz) and was normally attached to the 2nd Cavalry Division. Armoured battalions had two companies of 16 tanks – only the command tanks had wireless transmitters.

The Turkish army could be described as a First World War army in terms of equipment and doctrine. By the end of the war, Turkey had mobilised 16 corps with 55 divisions of 15,000 men. This included four mechanised and two armoured divisions. It also acquired some modern equipment from Britain and Germany, although, as we will see, changing the doctrine would be more challenging.

**Equipment**

In October 1939, Turkish officers described their weaponry as consisting of museum pieces and the soldier's rations consisted of bulgur wheat for breakfast, lunch and dinner.[4]

There were many infantry rifles in use, including Mausers, Mannlichers, Lee–Enfields, Martinis, Lebels and others. During the war, they shipped large numbers of these rifles to Germany to be bored to a standard 7.65mm calibre. In February 1940, the British

The Russian supplied T26 was the main tank in the pre-war armoured brigade. (Carl9311, CC BY-SA 4.0)

machine guns in the infantry regiments were mainly Maxim or Schwarzlose and some had stands for use as anti-aircraft machine guns.

There was little standardisation in the provision of artillery, which totalled some 600 field guns. Infantry guns were either 75mm Bofors or 65mm French with 75mm field guns and 105mm at divisional level and Skoda 150mm howitzers at corps level. Anti-tanks guns were horse-drawn 37mm Rheinmetall or SA-34 25mm, with British guns on order. Horse artillery was mainly Krupp 75mm with a few Schneider 75mm. Mountain artillery included 105mm Skoda guns and 75mm Krupp or Bofors. Anti-aircraft guns were mainly Vickers 75mm and 3.7inch guns, plus a few German 77mm and Japanese 76.2mm. Britain supplied Boys anti-tank rifles, although ammunition was limited.

The 1939 Anglo-French war materials credit included an order for 100 French Renault R.35 medium tanks, of which 50 had been delivered by March 1940. They also had 100 Soviet T26 light tanks, 15 British Mark VI and 20 Soviet T37 tankettes.[5] The armoured car battalion had 38 Soviet BA6 organised into two companies.[6] Turkey also took delivery of 12 Citroen-Kegresse two-seater light armoured cars in 1929. The motorised infantry battalions used Czech and Soviet trucks.

were asked to supply 150,000 rifles, which indicates the scale of the equipment requirements, even if an unrealistic expectation of what Britain could provide. Each infantryman carried 120 rounds with more in the company and regimental reserves. The medium

### Uniforms

The British handbook on the Turkish army describes officers as smartly dressed, not least because uniforms were often made by

Schwarzlose 7.92mm HMG. (Photo by Christoph T.)

Turkish pre-war anti-tank gun (German-made PAK 37) and field artillery. (Istanbul Military Museum, Author)

French supplied Renault R35 tank. (Photo by Author, US Army Ordnance Museum, Aberdeen)

French supplied Schneider 105mm field howitzer. (Photo by Author)

Model 1925 Turkish Army field cap. (via William Cobb)

private tailors. However, the rank and file are described as being provided with; 'very shoddy, ill-fitting clothes which in most cases, look extremely shabby, more especially in the east'.

Officers had a different home service or full dress uniform. It was a dark olive drab colour with a double stand-up collar, which had gorget patches of the colour of the arm of service. Badges of rank were shown on the shoulder straps. Trousers were of the same colour with a thin red stripe on the outside seams – a broader two inch stripe for generals.

The field service uniform was the same for all ranks. A rough, grey mixture, woollen serge uniform in winter and a khaki coloured canvas material in summer. The tunic was single-breasted with five metal buttons painted the same colour as the tunic. There were pantaloons or breeches for officers of the same material with butcher boots for the cavalry and cloth gaiters for the infantry, fastened down the side with eight zinc buttons.

The cap was the same colour and material, with a flap folded up and buttoned around the front above the short peak. Sometimes described as being like a jockey's cap. A cap badge consisted of a small brass crescent and star on a cloth background of the arm of service. A plain leather belt with a brass buckle was also worn.

The overcoat was single-breasted with five metal buttons down the front, made of the same material as the winter uniform. Arm of service colour was worn on the collar. Short sheepskin coats with the fur outwards were issued to sentries and certain specialist troops in winter.

BA-6 armoured car during a military parade in Ankara. (via William Cobb)

The British had a positive view of the Turkish soldier, albeit expressed in the colonial stereotypes of the period. The British army handbook says;

> The Turk is essentially a soldier and has possessed little aptitude for business … A strong trait in the national character is an intense loyalty to superior authority backed by an instinct of complete obedience. The Turkish soldier is notoriously hardy and patient and asks for little comfort. He is at his best in defence.[8]

Turkish officers conceded elements of this stereotype with one saying, 'An Anatolian mountain soldier is almost as steadfast as a British grenadier, almost as sturdy as a Yank, perhaps even as ferocious as a German and as patient as a Russian. He is all these at once and besides, he hardly needs as much food as a Chinese'.

In 1939, Lord Gort, the British Chief of the General Staff, took a particularly positive view of the Turkish Army. He told General Wavell that they were a 'formidable body of troops', who would not be overrun by the Germans. This reflected a broader positive

| Arm of Service | Colour |
|---|---|
| Generals | Scarlet |
| Staff Officer | Cherry |
| Infantry | Dark green |
| Cavalry | Light grey |
| Artillery | Dark blue |
| Engineers | Sky blue |
| Signal troops | Sky blue |
| Railway troops | Sky blue |
| Transport | Dark mauve |
| Supplies | Light mauve |

Officer rank badges made of gilt metal were worn on shoulder straps for officers and as gold chevrons on a cloth of the arm of service above the elbow for senior NCOs. Other NCOs had a similar cloth patch with horizontal red stripes.

**Army Performance and Doctrine**

It is difficult to fairly assess the performance and morale of the Turkish army when it was untested in war. Most armies are prepared to fight the last war and war has a habit of challenging pre-war assumptions and doctrines, as the British and the French discovered in 1940. As Barno and Bensahel observe,[7] militaries need to be adaptable and demonstrate this within their doctrine, technologies and leaders. At the outset of the Second World War, the Turkish army was largely wedded to the German doctrine of the First World War and had outdated technology. Its leadership was older with a mindset rooted in their experience of the Greek-Turkish War 1919–1923.

| Rank | Badge |
|---|---|
| *Marezal* (Marshal) | Crescent and star with gilt border |
| *Orgeneral* (General) | Three horizontal bars above crescent and star |
| *Korgeneral* (Lieutenant-General) | Three horizontal bars with three stars above |
| *Tumgeneral* (Major-General) | Three horizontal bars with two stars above |
| *Tugbay* (Acting as Brigadier) | Two bars and three stars |
| *Albay* (Colonel) | Two bars and three stars |
| *Yarbay* (Lieutenant-Colonel) | Two bars and two stars |
| *Binbasi* (Major) | Two bars and one star |
| *Yuzbasi* (Captain) | One bar and three stars |
| *Uztegmen* (1st Lieutenant) | One bar and two stars |
| *Tegmen* (2nd Lieutenant) | One bar and one star |
| *Astegmen* (3rd Lieutenant) | One bar |
| *Bascavus* (Sergeant Major) | Four gold chevrons |
| *Bascavus Muavini* (Assistant Sergeant Major) | Three gold chevrons |
| *Cavus* (Sergeant) | Two gold chevrons or two red stripes |
| *Onbasis* (Corporal) | One red stripe |

view of Turkey's modernisation under Atatürk in the 1930s. A perception that would be punctured somewhat during the war and which showed that Britain had overestimated the pace and scale of change. However, the British analysis also pointed to the lack of formal education for NCOs who were usually regulars. Turkish officers were mainly recruited from the middle classes but there was no officer caste system in the social sense. Something an RAF staff officer seconded to the Turkish Staff College commented on favourably. Regular officers trained at Harbie Mektebi, the Turkish equivalent of Sandhurst or West Point, which moved from Istanbul to a new building in Ankara in 1936. They entered at age 15 and after graduation, served two years as a junior lieutenant. Promotion was slow, typically taking 15 years to reach the rank of captain.[9]

Doctrine was based on the German 1933 regulations, which followed the translation of German manuals into Turkish in 1921. During the War of Independence, the Turkish military had absorbed German experience on the Western Front. The Germans had trained Ottoman troops in the use of assault troop doctrines (Stormtroop tactics) and a special training school had been established at Maltepe in May 1917.[10] Smaller ones were established near Ankara called 'assault grounds' during the preparations for the Great Offensive in 1922. The Turkish translation of the German manual 'Attack in Position Warfare' was required reading by Turkish staff officers. This was developed by Kemal and his commanders, although they lacked the same levels of equipment, organisation and education of NCOs. In particular, the lack of squad leaders trained in mission-type tactics (*Auftragstaktik*) meant that Turkish divisions struggled to make deep penetrations, bypassing strong points.[11]

Turkish military journals of the 1930s regularly referenced the development of German military thinking and these links survived the defeat in the First World War. Most senior officers had been trained at the German staffed Ottoman War Academy and others, including İnönü, had served with German officers during the war. The Chief of Staff, Fevzi Çakmak, was an admirer of the Germans and his assistant, Asim Gündüz, was a friend of Field Marshall Wilhelm Keitel, Chief of the Armed Forces High Command (OKW) during the Second World War.[12] Younger officers studied

Field Marshal Fevzi Çakmak, Chief of the General Staff. (Public Domain)

in Germany during the 1930s and saw the growing military and economic power first hand. A point reinforced by technical instructors assigned to the Turkish army and teachers at the Staff Academy. However, Turkish officers and NCOs had not adopted the flexibility and initiative that was a key feature of the German system. Turkish staff officers travelled as observers to most of the main battlefronts with both sides during the war. German influence, while significant, should not be overstated as officers also trained in France and Britain and attended the major field exercises of the main military powers. During the war, the Turkish General Staff sent two delegations to Germany. The October 1941 delegation toured the Eastern Front and met Hitler, returning with an optimistic view of German success. The second in July 1943 arrived during the Battle of Kursk and reported less optimistically.

A key challenge for the army was the lack of mobility. There was only a single-track railway spanning the country from east to west and

Turkish and German officers inspecting a Panzer VI 'Tiger I'; KBZ HGr Northern Ukraine, 1943. (Bundesarchiv Bild 101I-704-0149-13A)

roads were generally poor. In any case, the army had too few and generally obsolete vehicles, which meant that units had to march with a supply train of horse-drawn wagons. War fuel supplies during the war could drop to one week's supply and were exposed to bombing raids. The Provisioning Directorate struggled to find supplies and transport and dealt daily with complaints from provincial governors and army commanders. The government sought to address this by giving the army precedence in economic plans. In February 1940, civilian rationing was introduced, prices fixed and extra workers were allocated to heavy industries. This led to a huge rise in the black market and counterfeit ration tickets.

The terrain also brought some advantages to the defender if the army was prepared to abandon Thrace and Istanbul. A politically challenging prospect that led to the maintenance of long-standing fortifications outside Istanbul. Before the Second World War, Atatürk prophetically compared the Maginot Line to a tomb that anyone could go around the edge of.[13] The Çatalca lines outside Istanbul could not be

The natural defences of the Çakmak Line can be seen from this aerial view of the lake of Büyük Çekmece Gölü. (Photo by Author)

Çakmak Line bunkers. (Photo by Author)

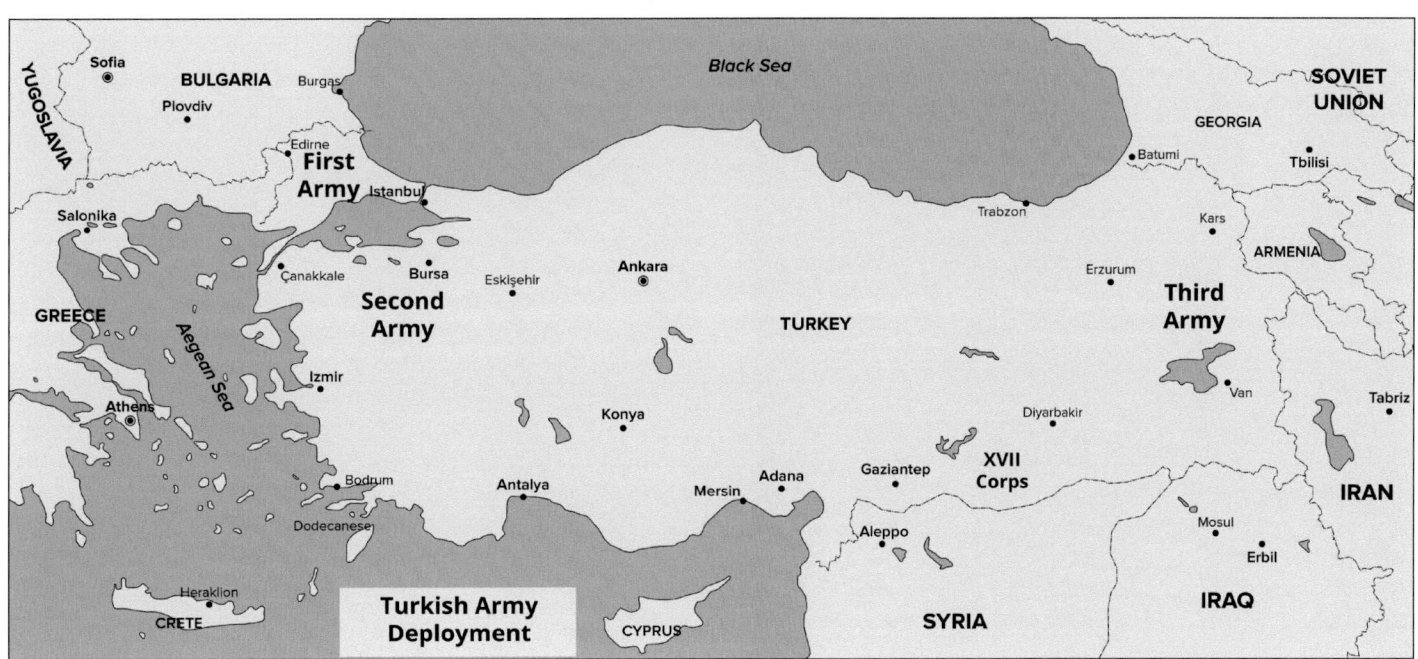
Turkish Army deployment. (Map by Author)

Kayseri aircraft factory (KTF) with a Polish PZL P-24C fighter produced by the PZL factory in Warsaw and under licence by KTF in 1936–1937. The P-24C series for Turkey consisted of 26 planes made by the PZL in Poland and 20 licenced ones by the KTF. (via William Cobb)

Hurricane MkIIc in Turkish service. (Albert Grandolini Collection)

1928 to three regiments in 1932 and to three brigades in 1939. Operational efficiency was not up to western European standards, although probably no worse than its immediate neighbours, Greece and Bulgaria. There was a serious shortage of mechanics and the reliance on imports would inevitably put pressure on spare parts. Pilot training included limited operational flying, with virtually no bad weather flying experience. The Allies estimated that the Turkish Air Force would last only a few days if invaded, due to a lack of fuel and spare parts.

Turkey made some limited efforts to establish an aircraft industry. Junkers started a factory in Kayseri in 1925, which was taken over by Curtis-Wright in the early 1930s but only produced a few planes.[15] The Nuri Demirag works, established in 1937, supplied training and liaison aircraft.

There was no shortage of pilots but their training was insufficient for the modern aircraft types they were starting to acquire. There was limited training in flying out of sight of land and in bad weather and it was also doubtful whether bombers could navigate and bomb with any degree of accuracy. Anti-aircraft defences were totally inadequate and a single air raid would have severely damaged communications and heavy industry. A large number of wooden buildings in Istanbul made it particularly vulnerable to modern incendiary bombs. An RAF staff officer working with the Turkish Air Force at the outbreak of war argued that 'the weakness of the Air Force was the determining influence in Turkish reluctance to go to war'.[16] He highlighted obsolete equipment, deficiencies in command and operational control. The maintenance organisation, based on a solitary repair factory at Kayseri, was unable to keep pace with flying wastage. Units lacked mechanics and maintenance personnel. General Staff officers admitted to him that their Air Force would disappear in a few days against a sizeable German formation.

Turkish Air Force officers wore a uniform similar to army officers, except the colour was dark blue. The jacket had an open collar with a white collared shirt and black tie. The cap badge was also similar but with double wings across the middle. Other ranks again wore a similar uniform to the army, except for the dark blue colour.

The air force was organised into three air brigades of two air regiments. Each regiment had two or more battalions, typically with two squadrons each.

flanked in the same way as the Bulgarians discovered during the First Balkan War. This is a naturally strong defensive position along a ridgeline that goes from the lake of Terkos Gölü in the north, to the lake of Büyük Çekmece Gölü on the Sea of Marmara in the south. Çakmak took a more positive view than Atatürk of the value of fixed fortifications having visited the Maginot Line. He persuaded the government to invest the equivalent of a whole year's concrete supply into the renamed Çakmak Lines in 1938–1939. To this day, you can see dozens of concrete bunkers along a 25 kilometre front.

Last-minute panic buying was unlikely to plug the gaps in equipment or encourage a change in doctrine. Even as late as 1944, the Military Academy were teaching the parts of the horse-drawn carriage.[14] However, this was also true for most of its neighbours in the Balkans and the Middle East and even the Germans heavily relied on horse drawn transport.

**Turkish Air Force**

The Turkish air force only became a separate branch of the Turkish armed force in January 1944. At the outbreak of the Second World War, it was short of modern aircraft and infrastructure. Efforts had been made to rapidly expand the air force from three battalions in

> **Sabiha Gökçen** was the world's first female fighter pilot. She was one of Mustafa Kemal Atatürk's 13 adopted children. As women were not enrolled in the war academies, she received special education at the Tayyare Mektebi Aviation School in Eskisehir and then joined the 1st Air Regiment in 1937. She took part in military operations in the Dersim rebellion and then became a flight instructor until her retirement in 1952. Throughout her career in the Turkish Air Force, she flew 22 different types of aircraft for more than 8,000 hours, 32 hours of which were active combat and bombardment missions.
>
>
>
> Sabiha Gökçen (centre) in uniform. (Public Domain)

The Turkish Air Force deployment in the summer of 1940 was as follows:

- Eskisehir: 20 Heinkel III, 20 Fairey Battle, 10 Lysanders.
- Kütahya: 24 Hurricane, 24 Morane 406.
- Izmir: 24 Curtis Hawk, 31 Blenheim, five Walrus, four Southampton, 10 Lysander.
- Corlu: 20 Martin B10, 24 PZL 24.
- Istanbul: 10 Lysander.
- Diyarbekir: 35 Vultee V-11.

The Air Force had 237 additional aircraft not allocated to operational units. These were used for training or kept in reserve. A large number of modern aircraft were on order in 1940, including 50 Morane M.S.406 (30 delivered) from France and 25 Anson, 50 Spitfires and 34 Magisters, from Britain. Only two Spitfires and two Ansons were delivered. Some of these aircraft would have been used to establish an air regiment at a new airbase at Erzincan.

During the war, the Air Force sent many pilots to Britain for training. Fourteen died in accidents and at least one went as a passenger on a bombing mission over Germany. Turkey adopted British radar and air signalling systems during the war.

The Turkish Air Force received large numbers of new aircraft during the war, including:

- Fighters: Supermarine Spitfire Mk. I, V, IX and XIX, Hawker Hurricane Mk. I and II, Morane-Saulnier M.S.406, Curtiss P-40 Tomahawk and Kittyhawk, Curtiss Falcon CW-22R/B, P-47D Thunderbolt and the German Focke Wulf FW-190-A3
- Bombers: Fairey Battle Mk. I, Consolidated B-24D Liberator, Bristol Blenheim Mk. IV and V, Bristol Beaufort, Bristol Beaufighter Mk. I and X, Martin 187 Baltimore, de Havilland DH.98 Mosquito Mk. III and IV, Douglas B-26B and C Invader
- Transport and others: Avro Anson Mk. I, Westland Lysander Mk. I and Douglas C-47A and B Dakota

**Turkish Navy**

The Turkish Navy suffered most of all from the financial restrictions placed on the new republic. A British naval attaché reported in 1937 that, 'Judged by the standards of modern navies, however small, the condition of the fleet is far from satisfactory'.[17] He suggested that they had not been updated since the First World War, which was not accurate and 'were defenceless against air attack', which was probably largely correct. There were around 800 officers and 4,000 men in the navy.

In the early days of the Republic, the focus was on building a limited coastal navy with the dominant army treating the navy as an extension of land operations. Security considerations in the Kurdish regions also gave priority to aircraft over ships. Tensions with Greece in the Aegean ensured some limited funds were made available for modernising the battlecruiser, *Yavuz,* as well as purchasing mines and submarines. Mussolini's speech on Italian expansion in 1934, put some focus back on the navy, although budget pressures limited expenditure.

The modest budget focused on the defence of the Dardanelles, backed up by a mobile force led by the First World War battlecruiser *Yavuz* (ex *Goeben*) and four destroyers. The main naval base was at Gölcük in the Sea of Marmara.

The inclusion of ships built in Italy may appear surprising given the state of Turkish-Italian relations. However, this reflects a period of positive relations after the Treaty of Neutrality and Reconciliation in 1928. Italy agreed to provide Italian shipbuilders with a

| Ship | Type | Notes |
|---|---|---|
| *Yavuz* | Battle Cruiser | ex-*Goeben* modernised 1930 |
| *Hamidieh* and *Medjedieh* | Cruiser | Built 1903 using for training and minelaying |
| Two Adatepe or Kocatepe class | Destroyer | Modern design. Built in Genoa 1931 |
| Two Tinaztepe class | Destroyer | Modern design. Built in Trigoso 1931 |
| Two Peyk-i-Sevket class | Torpedo cruiser | Built in Germany 1906. Rebuilt 1936 |
| Two Birindci class | Submarine | Built in 1926 at Feyenoord |
| *Sakarya* | Submarine | Built 1931 in Italy |
| *Gur* | Submarine | Built in Spain 1934. Sold to Turkey. |
| Three Atilay class | Submarine | German design 1938 onwards |
| Three Isa Reis class | Minesweeper | Built 1911–1912 |
| *Nusret* and *Intibah* | Minesweeper | Built 1912 and 1886 |
| *Atak* | Minesweeper | Built 1938 |
| Dogan class | MTB | Bought from Italy in 1938 |

Turkish Battlecruiser *Yavuz* (ex-SMS *Goeben*) at Istanbul. (US Navy, Public Domain)

Turkish minesweeper, *Nusret*, recommissioned as a diving ship and tender in 1939. It laid 26 mines in the Dardanelles during February 1915, which sank three British and French warships. This replica *Nusret* is displayed in Çanakkale by the shore of the Dardanelles. (Author)

financial guarantee for up to 70 percent of the value of a Turkish order.[18] This added to Greek concerns, which were alleviated by a Greek naval order in 1929. The Friendship Treaty between Turkey and Greece in 1930 included a protocol to end the naval arms race in the Aegean. In 1929 the Turkish navy sent junior officers to Italy for training.

At the outbreak of war there was a ten-year plan to expand the fleet to one battle cruiser, two cruisers, two old cruisers, eight destroyers and 20 submarines, together with the necessary ancillary vessels. Ships were on order from Britain and Germany but were not delivered due to the outbreak of war. The navy had requested eight destroyers, eight submarines, four escorts and a range of smaller ships and equipment. Two Royal Navy I class destroyers were delivered in 1942 (named TCG *Demirhisar* and TCG *Sultanhisar*). Ten Thorneycroft MTBs were built in Turkey by 1942.

There was one battalion of marines. The Navy also had command of two naval aircraft squadrons equipped with Supermarine Walrus Mk.II and Supermarine Southampton Mk II aircraft.

Serhat Guvenc, in his study of the Republican Navy concludes that the process of building a navy in Turkey mirrored the state of relations with major European powers.[19] Budget limitations and supplier issues limited its growth in the early years. Ironically, the ships received from Italy in the early 1930s represent the largest contribution to Turkish naval efforts. This could not be sustained by the outset of the war, even though domestic political conditions and military thinking were more conducive to naval expansion.

# 3
# THREATS AND OPPORTUNITIES

Turkey faced a range of threats at the outbreak of war. The German and Soviet invasions of Poland reinforced the importance of the Straits between Europe and Asia. However, both Germany and, to a lesser extent, the Soviet Union had weak navies. Italy did have a strong navy and still occupied the Dodecanese islands off the Turkish coast. Eastern Turkey was protected by mountains from the Soviet Union, which favoured the defence. The border with the Middle East was also rugged, although the threat from the current mandate countries (France and Britain) was of less concern.

The new Turkish Republic had limited ambitions to recover former Ottoman territories, particularly those not occupied by ethnic Turks. The exception was some islands, Hatay province in Syria and it also would have liked a more defensible border in Thrace.

## Thrace

Turkey's European border in the Balkans was the remnant of the once-great Ottoman Empire, which at its height stretched to the walls of Vienna. Turkish Thrace had been salvaged at the end of the Second Balkan War and defended during the First World War and the Greek-Turkish War of 1919–1922. This border was where Turkey faced traditional enemies, Bulgaria and Greece.

Given the vicious nature of the recent war, Greece would be the obvious threat to Turkey in this region. However, they had settled their differences with border agreements and population exchanges. The Greco-Turkish Treaty of 1930, strengthened in 1933, gave mutual guarantees as to the 'inviolability of their common frontiers' (Article 1). Greece did have separate claims over its borders with Bulgaria along the Rhodope Mountains. A further treaty in 1938 bound the two countries to safeguard their respective neutrality by opposing the use of its territory by another power to move troops or equipment. This treaty did not commit Turkey to give Greece military assistance if attacked by a non-Balkan power. Greece was also given a limited commitment by Britain and France to come to their aid following the Italian invasion of Albania in 1939.

While Bulgaria had been on the same side as Turkey in the First World War, both Greece and Turkey regarded Bulgaria as a threat. The Greeks had reached an agreement with Bulgaria over the treatment of minorities in 1924,[1] but Macedonia, which also involved Yugoslavia, remained a potential area of conflict. The Turks also coveted the Sakar massif, which dominated the Turkish city of Edirne from Bulgaria. Defeated in the Second Balkan War, Bulgaria never fully accepted the borders imposed by the Peace Treaty of Neuilly in 1919. Bulgaria avoided commitments to other Balkan states and adopted a largely isolationist or, as some argue,[2] a divide and rule policy. For example, on 20 November 1938, Kiosseivanoff, the Bulgarian premier, addressing the Parliament, affirmed that his government would endeavour 'without rest, to improve the friendly relations with Yugoslavia and Turkey, while [they] would continue [their] efforts to accomplish the satisfactory solution of the pending issues with the other two neighbours, Rumania and Greece'.

Turkey made diplomatic efforts to get Bulgaria to join a Balkan bloc in 1940 without success. The Bulgarian premier did give an assurance of neutrality in case of aggression against a Balkan state. King Boris later undermined this in discussions with the Greek ambassador and Kiosseivanoff was forced to resign in February 1940, to be replaced by the more pro-German Filov.

Bulgaria's foreign policy remained focused on retrieving the borders similar to those achieved at the 1878 Treaty of San Stefano. That aim threatened Greece, Yugoslavia and Turkey and gave the Axis more bargaining chips than the Allies when both came looking for support in 1940. Germany was also Bulgaria's largest trading partner and took most of its exports.[3] In return, they were able to purchase armaments from Germany that were not available from domestic sources. As with Turkey, Britain did not need, nor could it compete with German prices and consequential economic dominance.

King Boris III of Bulgaria meeting Adolf Hitler in 1941. (United States Holocaust Memorial Museum, courtesy of Perquimans County Library)

The Maritsa River forms most of the border between Turkey and Greece in Thrace. (Starliner, Public Domain)

Entrance to the Dardanelles at Cape Helles. (Photo by Author)

## Aegean and the Straits

Turkey was faced with potentially hostile states on islands very close to their coastline in both the Aegean and the Dodecanese.

The Straits were the traditional naval threat to the former Ottoman capital of Istanbul. The Arabs in AD717-18, the Fourth Crusade in 1204 and the Ottoman's siege in 1453, all highlighted the importance of sealing the Straits through the Dardanelles and Bosporus. Winston Churchill's, albeit disastrous, Gallipoli campaign in 1915 was a further reminder of the threat.

The Straits were not just important to Turkey. They were an international waterway of great military and economic significance to the countries of the Black Sea, not least the Soviet Union. At the Montreux Conference on the Dardanelles in 1936, the Soviet Union pressed for the Straits to be closed to warships. The final agreement did increase the naval security of the Soviet Union by excluding belligerent forces, although they remained dissatisfied. It allowed Turkey to control and militarise the Straits by abolishing the previous International Commission. The Soviet Union was allowed to sail surface naval units through the Straits in peacetime and in time, wartime, as long as Turkey remained neutral and the Soviet Union was non-belligerent. In either case, the Turkish government had to be notified in advance.

In the 1940 negotiations with Germany, the Soviet Union again emphasised the importance of the Straits and also sought assurances in relation to Bulgaria accessing the Straits in case of war. The British doubted that the dictators could reach an agreement over the Straits, although there were those in the Foreign Office who argued that this was possible because they needed access for different purposes. The Germans effectively leaked these discussions to Turkey in March 1941 as part of their attempts to bring Turkey into the Axis before the invasion of the Soviet Union. This led to a confirmation of the Montreux Convention and an assurance of no aggressive intentions by the Soviet Union to Turkey in August 1941. Recent work on the Soviet archives (August 1939 to June 1941) confirm Stalin's security concerns about a British threat to the Soviet Union via the Black Sea and the Caucasus, possibly in collaboration with Turkey.[4] In the autumn of 1940, Stalin offered territorial concessions to Bulgaria in return for Soviet military bases on the Straits. Unlikely though the threat may seem today, these concerns influenced Soviet policy throughout the war and beyond. They are mentioned in the memoirs of Khrushchev, Molotov and Stalin's security chief, Sergo Beria.

Turkey's maritime borders in the Aegean and the Mediterranean stretch some 1,200 miles. Control of the islands by a potential enemy also means controlling access to Turkey's two principal harbours, Istanbul and Izmir. Turkey did want to recover the Dodecanese Islands, mostly lost to Italy in 1912. The British were more sympathetic to Greek claims to the islands, which were realised in 1947, despite objections from Turkey. In 1940, the Turkish ambassador to London explicitly claimed the Dodecanese in response to a British request to allow the use of Turkish territorial waters to attack Italian shipping.[5] Turkish relations with Italy had thawed following the Treaty of Neutrality and Reconciliation in May 1928. This resulted in Turkish and then Greek warships being built in Italian shipyards. The 1930 Friendship Treaty with Greece included protocols that sought to end the naval arms race in the Aegean that neither country could afford. Relations with Italy deteriorated in 1932 when Turkey accepted loans from the Soviet Union rather than Italy because they came without interest. This was followed by a more aggressive Italian foreign policy and opposition to Turkey joining the League of Nations. The Balkan Pact (1934) and supporting sanctions against Italy for the invasion of Abyssinia were the final straw in relations, Turkey returned to its traditional concern over Italian aims on its borders.[6]

The North Aegean islands were also Ottoman territory until they were incorporated into Greece after the First Balkan War in 1912. While the populations were predominately Greek, they are strategically very close to the Turkish coast. Cyprus was an Ottoman territory until 1878, when it was transferred to Britain to develop a naval base to counter Russian aggression. Britain formally annexed it in 1914 when the Ottoman Empire allied with Germany. Twenty percent of the population were Turkish and they occasionally called for a union with Turkey, usually in response to the Greek population demanding a union with Greece. Britain considered giving Cyprus to Greece in 1940 but decided they did not want to alienate Turkey.

## Soviet Union

Ottoman Turkey had fought many wars with Imperial Russia over the centuries. While the focus of the conflict was usually in the Balkans, the eastern borders were the scene of many battles. In contrast, early relations between the Turkish Republic and the Soviet Union were generally good. The Soviets aided Turkey in its war with Greece with military advice, cash and equipment and ordered the Greek communists to undermine morale in the Greek army.[7]

The first treaty signed by the Turkish Republic in March 1921 was with the Soviet Union. This treaty settled the borders between the two countries that survive the modern period. The two countries recognised 'their solidarity in their struggle against imperialism, as well as the fact that any difficulty encountered by either of the two peoples would worsen the position of the other'. These words reflect the difficulties both countries faced at the time, a largely pragmatic, anti-imperialist rather than an ideological détente.

This treaty was followed by a treaty of neutrality, non-aggression and mutual consultation signed in Paris in 1925 and renewed 10 years later in 1935. Even Soviet concerns over the Straits were recognised, with Turkey offering to close them if the Soviet Union was attacked. There had even been negotiations for maintaining a Soviet fleet on the Aegean near the port of Izmir.[8] Efforts were made to soothe Soviet concerns about the scale of German involvement in Turkey. The Chief of Staff, known for his pro-German sympathies, was dispatched with a delegation to observe Red Army manoeuvres in 1935. Requests were made for more Soviet experts to work in Turkey and discussions about developing trading links. İnönü appears to have genuinely wanted to lessen Turkey's economic dependence on Germany and the Soviet approach mirrors similar discussions with Britain and France.[9]

As outlined in Chapter 1, the Soviet Union was seeking a new treaty with Turkey when France and Great Britain were finalising the 1939 declarations. These collapsed largely due to the Molotov-Ribbentrop Pact of August 1939. It has been argued that this pact caused a reversion to traditional Turkish concerns about Russia,[10] abetted by Nazi propaganda.

The Soviet Union did have claims in eastern Turkey, primarily the provinces of Kars and Ardahan, which had been conceded to Turkey in the 1921 treaty against Stalin's wishes. The Soviet foreign minister, Molotov, denied these rumours in October 1939, although he added that Turkey's pact with France and Britain was a 'hazardous line', which she would regret.[11] The Turks had noted how the Soviets had dealt with Poland and might respond similarly to Turkey. Turkey was also concerned that the Soviet Union was supporting Kurdish tribes in Eastern Turkey seeking independence. This was and remains to the present day, a major Turkish security concern. The Kurdish tribes occupied territory in Turkey and across the borders into Iran and Iraq. The bloody Dersim Rebellion of 1937–1938 was a recent reminder of what Atatürk had described as Turkey's most important interior problem.[12]

After Bulgaria joined the Axis, the Soviet Union pivoted again towards Turkey. A joint declaration in March 1941 stated, 'the reports appearing in the foreign press that, if Turkey were led to enter the war, the Soviets would take advantage of her difficulties to attack her in no way corresponds to the position of the Soviet Union'. This remained the Soviet position throughout the war, until 1945 when new demands were made and the two countries came close to war.

Turkey's border with the Soviet Union became significant again in 1941–1942 as the German armies entered the Caucasus. Britain described this as the 'Northern Front' in the Middle East when Rommel was threatening the region from Libya.

**Middle East**

Relations with bordering states in the Middle East were reasonably stable, based on the Saadabad Pact of 1937 signed by Turkey, Iran, Iraq and Afghanistan. This was a non-aggression pact to last for five years, automatically extended in 1943 because none of the signatories denounced it.

Turkey's main land border in the Middle East was with Syria, a French mandate. The dispute over Hatay province (Alexandretta) was settled in July 1938 prior to the Franco-Turkish Pact of Friendship. The 'line the sand' deal between Britain and France after the First World War defined imperial spheres of influence and fragmented the region into small and manageable national states.[13] This proved as difficult and costly for the mandate powers as it was unjust and deadly for the people of the region. The French *mission civilitrice* was anything but civilised for those killed or made homeless in often random punishment bombings of villages suspected of supporting insurgents. These revolts were often led by former Ottoman officers, although they received little assistance for Turkey.

The other main border was with Iraq, a limited British mandate and the pact with Britain left an ally on that border. Turkey had sought sovereignty over Mosul, valuable for its oil deposits but the Court of International Justice decided in favour of Britain. Turkey received some compensation and swallowed the defeat for the time being. In July 1940, the Iraq minister of justice approached the German ambassador to Turkey, seeking German support in declaring independence from Britain. Papen got an ambiguous response to his question regarding the participation of the Iraqi army in the war, so he sent him away without encouragement.

Turkey and Persia had fought many wars over the centuries but outstanding border disputes had been resolved by 1914 under the Treaty of Erzurum 1847. Persia had started a modernisation programme under the rule of Reza Khan from 1925, which he renamed Iran in 1935. The country had good trading relations with Germany but declared neutrality at the outbreak of the Second World War. German nationals held important positions in strategic industries and when the Shah refused to expel them, Britain and the Soviet Union invaded and occupied the country in August 1941.

The Germans had a more active relationship with the Grand Mufti of Jerusalem. He was opposed to the British mandate in Palestine and Jewish immigration and had good relations with Arab leaders across the region. He fled Palestine for Syria after inciting riots but the Allies did not take stronger action for fear of alienating Muslim opinion. Both Axis partners were sceptical of the practical support the Grand Mufti could offer and at this stage of the war offered only general declarations in favour of Arab independence. Papen's advice to Berlin was not to encourage Arab nationalism for fear of alienating Turkey. He argued that Turkey remained Germany's only land bridge to the Middle East. The Italian's were more sceptical, taking the view that the Arabs could not be trusted.

**Internal Issues**

The Turkish government put the nation onto a war footing through the provisions of the 1940 National Defence Law, which granted sweeping powers over the means of production, prices and political expression. While such laws were common in the countries of Europe at war, such as the Bevin Boys in Britain, Turkey was non-belligerent.

During the war, the government used these powers to control cement factories, textile mills and mines. This included the main coal mines in the Zonguldak region and the Compulsory Paid Labour Act allowed a forced labour regime for men aged 16 and above. The area became the most populated region of Turkey during the war, with soldiers and criminals drafted in to make up the required numbers. Workers lost their rights to choose their workplace, wages, working hours and overtime. Safety standards were deplorable and 601 workers died from accidents and a further 2,901 were injured. While trade unions and collective action were banned, workers found many ways of subverting the system from within and productivity fell.[14]

The war economy meant most people suffered under the pressure of high inflation, the black market and food scarcity, while profiteering created a class of war, rich at the expense of real wages. Army conscription took male adults from the agricultural areas decreasing food production. Increasing defence expenditure resulted in the cancellation of investment plans in the industrial and transportation sectors. It was workers and peasants that bore the economic burden of the war.

Internal policies also impacted foreign affairs. In particular, the burden of a wealth tax in 1942, the *Varlik Vergisi*, mainly fell on Greeks and Jews. It was designed to address war profiteering but corrupt officials used it to dispossess non-Muslim minorities, with many threatened with internment in labour camps. This infuriated the Greek government in exile and the US State Department, who warned the *Varlik* could disrupt American-Turkish relations. It even punctured the usually pro-Turkish British propaganda with memories of nineteenth century disputes with the 'terrible Turks'. It was also a reminder that Turkey was not a functioning democracy in a war that latterly was defined as a struggle for democracy.

# 4
# SALONIKA FRONT

On 15 October 1915, French and British troops began disembarking in the Greek port of Salonika (modern-day Thessaloniki). After the dismal failure of the Gallipoli campaign, the plan was to advance through Macedonia and support the Serbian army. A week, later Bulgaria joined the Central Powers and attacked Serbia. The Entente had arrived too late to save Serbia but the Salonika or Macedonian campaign dragged on for the remainder of the First World War. The final offensive in September 1918, knocked Bulgaria out of the war. It allowed French, Italian, Serbian and British troops to advance up the Vardar Valley, liberate Serbia and the capitulation of Austria-Hungary. Meanwhile, British forces advanced towards Turkey, which led to the Turks signing an armistice at Mudros.

The Salonika campaign is one of the less well-known campaigns of the First World War. The British troops were even described as 'The gardeners of Salonika',[1] and there are no streets in Paris named after the French victories on this front. While many dismissed the campaign as a sideshow, the German memory was somewhat different. When Hindenburg asked the German government to sue for peace on 3 October 1918, he claimed it was the defeat of Bulgaria which precipitated the collapse of the Central Powers.

At the outbreak of the Second World War, German strategic thinking had not forgotten the Salonika campaign. Hitler remembered this lesson throughout the war as he once said, 'Salonika had been the beginning of Germany's defeat last time'.[2] Neither had Winston Churchill, who in 1927 argued that it was this front that started the collapse of the Central Powers.[3]

While the panzers rolled into Poland, British strategy was fixed there and on the Italian threat in the Mediterranean. Turkey and to a lesser degree Greece, was viewed as guarding the Middle East against German, Italian and even Russian aggression. However, despite a desire to keep out of the Balkans, Britain and France were already committed to guaranteeing both Greece and Romania since April 1939. The Greek decision was something of panic response to Albania's Italian invasion and was important to Britain's maritime strategy in the Mediterranean. Romania was a French project driven by rumours of a German threat. It was hoped that Turkey could be persuaded to defend Romania and the British offered Turkey a similar guarantee if they would guarantee Romania. In practical terms, only Turkey or the Soviet Union could provide immediate military support if the Germans invaded. However, Turkey was not biting. They eventually agreed to start negotiations in May 1939 on the basis of a vague agreement to cooperate but there was no deal by the time war broke out.

Germany had strong cards to play in the Balkans. They had better economic and trade ties and were prepared to offer a wide range of border revisions. The Balkans were not part of Hitler's Lebensraum; its allotted role was to be a source of mineral and agricultural resources and a market for German manufactured goods. In contrast, the Allies were committed to the status quo and had no use for Turkish tobacco or Romanian wheat. The Allies did have admirers amongst the elites, memories of First World War alliances and royal contacts. However, that weighed lightly on the balance sheets, particularly when the war was going well for the Axis.

In the summer of 1939, British policy was focused on creating a neutral Balkan bloc based on the Balkan Entente of 1934. They were particularly keen not to irritate Mussolini, who (it is often forgotten) did not declare war until France was effectively defeated in 1940. Chamberlain was convinced he

British war memorial at Doiran, one of the main battlefields of the Salonika Campaign. (Photo by Author)

could separate Mussolini from Hitler.[4] Romania was supportive of this approach and there was some encouragement from Turkey. The Entente aimed to counter Bulgaria's territorial claims but they would be an essential player in creating a new bloc. However, Bulgaria was unlikely to engage without recognition of its territorial claims.

From a military perspective, the British Chiefs of Staff took the view that Balkan neutrality should help Italian neutrality,[5] limit the drain on shipping and restrict the area of military operations until British resources were fully developed. They pointed to Germany's interior lines, 'The railway will always beat the ship, particularly if that ship has to go round by the Cape!' They also preferred giving arms to Turkey over Romania. Largely because Turkey was more likely to be able to hold out against the Germans and the Russians and they could more easily be supplied, 'Turkey is the only country among the Balkan powers that is capable of resisting a first class power and that not until she has received considerable material support'.

The Balkan Entente met in Belgrade in 1940 and agreed to hold staff talks to prepare for mutual defence. Although they did not participate, even Bulgaria made positive noises about being a member of the Balkan family of nations.[6] Britain viewed Turkey as being the base of this bloc. However, the fall of France and the subsequent territorial revisions between Hungary, Russia and Bulgaria, largely at Romania's expense, meant the British were chasing fewer and fewer allies in the Balkans, with Turkey backing off as well.

While the British pursued diplomacy, the French were keen on finding somewhere to attack Germany other than on their own borders and assumed that the war would again stabilise on the Western Front. Memories of the great advance into central Europe from Salonika in 1918 drove plans to repeat this approach in 1940. The driving force was the French General Weygand, who commanded French forces in the Levant. The British Government and the Chiefs of Staff were hostile to the idea for fear of driving Italy into the war. The War Cabinet minute (26 November 1939) describes the Weygand plan; 'He was believed to have rather far-reaching ideas for staff conversations with the various Balkan countries'.[7]

The exception was Churchill, who, as First Lord of the Admiralty, said, 'We should do everything possible to marshal Yugoslavia, Greece, Turkey, Bulgaria and Rumania against the German threat'. Churchill also demonstrated his soft spot for Mussolini, arguing in Cabinet that if 'Greece, Rumania and Yugoslavia were to come in on our side, it was even possible that Italy might too'.[8]

Weygand's plan was for five divisions to land at Salonika to create a base there and started signing himself, 'Commander in Chief of the East Mediterranean Theatre of Operations'. The Yugoslavs pointed out that the French only had three divisions in Syria, whereas the Germans had 48 available for deployment in the Balkans. Prince Paul complained that the French were failing to keep these talks confidential. They were also concerned about Bulgaria because assistance to Romania meant marching across Bulgaria, which meant they were more concerned about the Allies than the Axis compromising their neutrality.

The British Chiefs of Staff argued that Salonika was not a good port, had poor communications northwards and the area was malarial. In the First World War, the army's Salonika newspaper was called 'The Mosquito'. They calculated that 20–24 divisions would be required to defend Salonika and the War Cabinet Joint Planning Committee decided that no British divisions would be available.[9] Britain would also have to provide divisions for the defence of Turkey and even a neutral Turkey would add to the problems defending Salonika. They claimed the defence of Salonika required 12–14 French divisions, which the British hoped would discourage the French. The British would also have to provide much of the shipping, which they believed gave them a veto. British objections did not stop Weygand from developing his plan. The French reported that Greece had agreed to French officers inspecting aerodromes and creating supply dumps. The Yugoslav General Staff agreed to supply information on communications and transport. The disaster in Norway reinforced the importance of large scale air support and anti-aircraft defences, which the Allies did not have available to allocate to the Salonika project.

Turkey was not a passive observer to this activity and signed the Anglo-French alliance in October 1939. In addition to the Treaty, Britain exchanged a note with Turkey that recognised her need for support if hostile forces reached her 'security zone'. As the Chiefs of Staff pointed out,[10] this would include the Bulgarian border and could involve Britain in a purely Balkan squabble, as the Treaty had a 15 year term. However, they and the Foreign Office believed it was a necessary risk to achieve the Treaty. A conference was held in Ankara on 20–21 October 1939, at which the Turkish armed forces set out to their French and British counterparts (Weygand and Wavell) their material requirements in the event of war. This is confirmed in a memo dated 22 November 1939 from Marshal Fevzi Çakmak.[11] His priorities were for tanks and anti-aircraft guns to be provided 'with the least possible delay'. He declined military missions in the country 'as inopportune and likely to raise the suspicions of the Russians', although British notes indicate this was agreed, so long as they were small in number.

The British Middle East Command conference (27 October 1939) adds some further detail.[12] Naval commanders were concerned about shipping to Salonika, particularly if Italy joined the war. They also had concerns over the adequacy of Turkish naval preparations. The RAF were concerned about the supply of aviation fuel through poor railroads from the Middle East and the suitability of Turkish airfields allocated to the RAF. The army wanted to discourage Turkish plans to attack the Dodecanese islands as their assessment was that they 'were very heavily fortified in all respects'. Wavell in his memo to the Chief of the General Staff, was broadly supportive of supplying material support to Turkey. Turkey also agreed to send a Colonel to Greece to liaise over the Salonika area.

The Greek position is documented in response to the Turkish General Staff.[13] They were sceptical that four to five Allied divisions would be of much use. Like Turkey, the priority was aircraft, air defences and naval assistance, otherwise, transport would be impossible. No troops could be landed until the Greek army had mobilised. Greece was also concerned about an attack from Bulgaria, who they claimed were receiving assistance from Germany. Interestingly, they considered an attack by Italy from Albania as 'not at all probable'.

Turkey also took some internal steps to prepare for any involvement in the war. As noted earlier, legislation gave extraordinary powers to the government, including a declaration of war and the total or partial mobilisation of the armed forces. This law remained in force until 15 June 1960. On 2 December 1940, a blackout in cities was initiated by the government.

Weygand's plans were not limited to Salonika. He also planned an airborne expedition to Romania, claiming that the French Air Commander in Chief had promised him as many aircraft as needed. The British Air Attaché in Bucharest reported that this plan had 'been received with terror' by the Romanian General Staff. Given the French had only two Airborne Infantry Groups (601st and 602nd)

Baku oilfield. (via William Cobb)

Royal Navy aircraft carriers in the Mediterranean. (Priest L C (Lt) Royal Navy Official Photographer)

of the French army,[17] argues that Gamelin was privately opposed to the Salonika and saw it as a way of keeping Weygand away from the Western Front.

The British were not beyond eastern adventures at this time. Churchill put a proposal to the War Cabinet in October 1939 to insert submarines into the Black Sea to interrupt Russian oil supplies to Germany.[18] Plans were also drawn up to bomb Russian oilfields in Baku, in effect a declaration of war against the Soviet Union. Such an attack would require flying over Turkey. The French claimed to have the Turkish Foreign Minister's tacit agreement to this,[19] although he recommended that Turkey should not formally be asked so that they could plead a fait accompli to the Russians. This became known as the Massigli Affai,[20] after the French Ambassador to Turkey who prepared the report. He was subsequently sacked by the Vichy Government and later became the effective Free French foreign minister. These papers included a secret protocol between France and Great Britain, which set out the details of the operation. The French and British General Staff agreed to assemble units that aimed to destroy 35 percent of Soviet oil fields over a six day aerial campaign involving 100 aircraft.

These plans were abandoned when Finland

in 1939, this movement of troops would require large numbers of transport aircraft and airfields. The French did promise Romania machine guns and tanks together with '20 aeroplanes of the most recent pattern',[14] and asked the British to match this offer. However, the French Commander in Chief, General Gamelin, indicated to the British that he did not believe Romania would withstand German pressure.[15]

Gamelin favoured an initiative in the Balkans over Scandinavia. His diary on 10 March 1940 notes, 'An initiative in the Balkans would be much more satisfactory to us than an enterprise in Scandinavia. Yugoslavia, Rumania, Greece and Turkey would give us the help of about 100 divisions. The forces that the Germans would be compelled to detach from the Western Front would be about the same dimensions'. As the Italian historian Mario Servi points out,[16] Gamelin was talking nonsense. 100 outdated Balkan divisions were not the equivalent of 100 German divisions. Ernest May in his study

surrendered to the Soviets before the Allies could intervene, which removed the risk of Soviet retaliation in the Middle East. However, the Germans sent captured French papers on the project to the Soviets to show that only German victories had saved Baku from British attack and tacit Turkish connivance. The Turkish government vigorously denied claiming that they consented and mounted a media campaign to ridicule it. Saracoğlu met the Soviet ambassador to deny the story as German propaganda but the Turkish Cabinet considered sacking him if there was a risk that it could lead to war with the Soviet Union.

The British were concerned that it would give the Turks an excuse for not coming into the war. It also did little to aid later British diplomatic overtures to the Soviet Union who required assurances that Baku would not be attacked from Iran or Turkey. The Soviets eventually took a relaxed view of the Turkish role, probably reflecting their policy of improving relations with Turkey in light of German

Italian battleship *Roma* in 1940. (Albert Grandolini Collection)

advances. Although at the time, they mobilised some 10,000 troops on the Turkish border in the Caucasus, which alarmed the Turkish government enough to respond by sending reinforcements to Kars. The German release of the papers did little to improve Turkish-German relations but they well understood Turkish concerns about the Soviet Union and Nazi propaganda was used to exploit this view.

Churchill, now back in the Cabinet as First Lord of the Admiralty, was quick to propose naval support for Turkey in the case of an attack by the Soviet Union.[21] As in the First World War, he was an 'Easterner', supporting a second front in the Balkans. A Cabinet Committee rejected sending land and air support but did authorise the Royal Navy to enter the Black Sea in such numbers as to deter the Soviets. This was a huge commitment that risked war with the Soviet Union and Germany, albeit only in the case of actual hostilities. It is also doubtful whether the Royal Navy could have delivered. The Soviet Black Sea fleet was 350 miles from the Straits compared to 850 miles for a sufficient Royal Navy fleet to get there. In light of the subsequent Soviet contribution to the Allied victory, this all appears absurd. However, in 1940, Turkey was deemed significantly more important to British interests than the Soviet Union.

The German invasion of France ended the Salonika project, with Weygand being recalled to the home front. The British claimed the planning was inadequate and unrealistic and they wanted to focus on safeguarding their Mediterranean routes to Malta and Egypt. They also placed a higher priority on defending Turkey and the Straits. The Chiefs of Staff had devised three different plans for Turkey by 1940. Operation Leopold involved establishing 30 British observer groups in Turkey. Operation Tiger would have inserted three fighter squadrons into mainland Turkey. Finally, Operation Bear involved an air defence programme and five squadrons of aircraft capable of attacking targets in the Balkans. None of these materialised as the Turks refused the 'help' being offered and in any case, many in Britain argued that supplying Turkey would damage the Western Front. The Treasury again pointed out that money and equipment were being provided to a country that might collaborate if the Italians attacked them and would not if the Russians were against them. The War Office shared the Treasury's scepticism; trust in Turkey was not high. There was even the suggestion that the Polish navy could be deployed in the Black Sea to intercept German oil supplies from Batumi in the Soviet Union because Poland was not a signatory to the Montreux Convention.

Mussolini announced that Italy would join the war on 10 June 1940 with what President Roosevelt would describe, as a stab in the back. He hoped for a short war, recognising that Italy was not ready for a long drawn out conflict with an army largely equipped with weapons left over from the First World War and a third-rate industrial base. The navy and air force were in a reasonable state of preparation and training, although liaison between them was poor. On 7 June, the Italian Admiralty ordered all merchant ships to reach Axis countries or neutral ports if that was not possible. This late recall resulted in the loss of 218 ships, about one-third of the merchant marine, a loss that would have profound consequences for the Italian war effort.

In practice, Britain put more effort into the Balkans and Turkey because of the threat to the Middle East, than they did in supporting Poland. Ironically, as we will see later, the Americans were to take a similar position to the 1940 British view when Churchill revisited the indirect approach later in the war. The Mediterranean was a vital thoroughfare to Britain's oil interests in the Middle East, which without it, would have to travel via the Cape. London to Alexandria via the Mediterranean was 3,097 miles; via the Cape, it was 11,608 miles, a difference of 8,511 miles. Control of the Suez Canal was secured through the Egyptian Treaty of 1936, which allowed Britain to maintain a peacetime garrison of 10,000 men and 400 aircraft to protect it. Defences at the other end of the Mediterranean were weaker because the British were allied with the French, a cruelly exposed policy after the fall of France. Nonetheless, despite the need to defend the home islands, Britain committed significant resources to the Mediterranean, including two divisions and dismissed the suggestion that they should abandon the Mediterranean in favour of a Cape route strategy. This decision continued to impact British strategy throughout the war.

On 26 June 1940, the Turkish government rejected the Allied request to join the war. The somewhat tenuous basis for this was built on the French seeking an armistice and the possible intervention by the Soviet Union, which was not party to the treaty. The Molotov-

# 5
# THE BALKANS AND THE SOVIET UNION 1940–1941

The fall of France came as a shock to Turkey and while they claimed it was in the Allies interest not to spread the war into the Balkans, there was no escaping the breakdown of the formal alliance with Britain and France. Italy's entry into the war did not change that position, particularly when the British withdrew a planned offer to invade the Dodecanese Islands. The Turks were particularly annoyed at French approaches for them to enter the war, just when they were deciding to give up. The British decided to make the best of the situation, noting the benefits of neutrality while recognising that they may feel equally absolved of their obligations to Turkey. A British military study in July 1940 concluded that the Germans could conquer Turkey in 16 weeks; a position that significantly threatened the British position in the Middle East.

Greece and Yugoslavia also indicated they would not declare war against Italy. Yugoslavia did commit to supporting Greece if attacked on the mainland but not if the Italians attacked Crete or Corfu. Bulgaria was only interested in fighting for the Dobruja area of Romania and the British assessment was that any extension of the war to the Balkans would bring them into an alliance with Germany.

After failing to agree on mutual defence at the final meeting of the Balkan Pact in February 1940, the Turks concluded that there were limited prospects for the Balkan states, other than Greece, to resist the Axis.

The German ambassador to Turkey, von Papen, believed that Turkey would not have violated their treaty commitments unless they were preparing to join the Axis. He even claimed that President İnönü had told him Turkey was considering such a move.[1] Turkey was particularly concerned over the fate of the French fleet as that would give the Axis naval control of the Mediterranean. The British recognised that this might deprive Britain of any value as an ally or even push Turkey into the German camp.[2] This may have influenced the British decision to sink the French fleet, an action welcomed by Turkey.

Recent research based on the Turkish Diplomatic Archives (TDA) suggests that while İnönü appointed pro-German officials to negotiate with the Axis,[3] he sought to contain that spirit at home. For example, When the Turkish Ambassador to Berlin, Hüsrev Gerede, made his pro-Nazi tendencies too explicit, he was twice reprimanded. He was recalled in August 1941 for making a pro-Nazi speech and dismissed in 1942 after publishing an article that celebrated Germany and Turkey's cooperation in the First World War.

Papen's optimistic assessment of Turkey's position led to a sceptical Ribbentrop and the German High Command allocating 21 million Turkish pounds worth of credits for weaponry to Turkey. The Italians were not impressed and made some vague commitments to Arab independence to drive a wedge between Germany and Turkey.

Canon de 75 M (montagne) modèle 1919 Schneider (75mm mle.1919) was a French mountain gun used extensively by the Greek Army in the Greek-Italian war. (Photo by Author, Athens War Museum)

## Italian Invasion of Greece

The Italian invasion of Albania in April 1939 faced minimal resistance, which was just as well, given poor Italian planning. Albania was incorporated into the Italian state and received an army of occupation commanded by Visconti Prasca. The Italian Foreign Minister Ciano looked for opportunities to exploit their position in Albania into an invasion of Yugoslavia or Greece and various territorial claims were made on behalf of Albania in Epirus. He attempted to reassure the sceptical Chief of the General Staff, Marshall Badoglio, that the timing was right because Greece was isolated and Turkey or Yugoslavia would not move.[4] Italian influence over Bulgaria was more limited than they believed and King Boris declined to join in because he was concerned that Turkey might attack Bulgaria.

Greek-Albania border. The main Italian thrust came down this route. (Photo by Author)

The Italian sinking of the Greek navy's biggest active warship, the cruiser Elli,[5] left the Greeks in no doubt of what was to come. The Greek Prime Minister, Ioannis Metaxas, quietly called up the 8th and 9th Divisions to the Epirus front. Metaxas had not sought war with the Axis. He had been trained in Germany and had spent many years in Italy. Ideologically his regime was similar to Mussolini's, although he had no significant territorial claims and had established good relations with Turkey. However, he was a pragmatist who recognised that Germany and Italy, not Britain, were the greatest threat to his country. He confidently declared, 'We are ready. We will defeat them'.

The original Italian plan (known as Contingency G) was a limited territorial expansion into the Epirus region for which the nine Italian divisions in Albania were deemed sufficient. However, this was expanded in a second phase to the total occupation of Greece at a meeting only two weeks before the invasion, at which the naval and air force chiefs were not even present. The Chief of the General Staff, Marshall Badoglio, who had previously indicated muted objections to the war, argued that 20 divisions would be required. Visconti Prasca asked for only three extra mountain divisions and some support units.

For such a modest army to be successful required several favourable factors, including; strategic and tactical surprise; a supporting invasion by Bulgarian forces; diversionary attacks on the poorly defended mainland; massive air support; and treachery in the Greek armed forces. However, the Greeks knew the approximate date of the invasion, which meant the Greek army was well established in the invasion area with the possibility of shifting reinforcements when Bulgarian neutrality became clear. No diversionary attacks were planned (even the island attacks were called off at the last moment) and a winter offensive coupled with negligible air planning minimised the value of Italian air superiority.[6] Despite optimistic views expressed by commanders in Albania and substantial investment in bribes, there was no evidence that Greek forces would collapse due to internal dissent.

The Italian offensive was launched on 28 October in driving rain that deprived the army of air cover. Rapidly rising rivers and mud tracks resulted in slow progress, with Greek screening forces falling back onto prepared positions. With the Italian offensive grinding to a halt, the Greeks counterattacked in the north and made spectacular advances in freezing conditions, pushing the Italians back off the mountains exposing the key valley town of Koritsa, which was abandoned on 21 November. Italian reinforcements were thrown into the line piecemeal, often without supporting arms and into a chaotic command structure. The loss of Koritsa and Erseke exposed the left flank of the 11th Army on the coast, which was forced to retreat deep into Albania whilst being vigorously counterattacked by fresh Greek divisions. By 10 January, the Klisura junction had been captured and Italian units only managed to stabilise the line south of the port of Vlone.

The Italians again reinforced up to a total of 28 divisions totalling 526,000 men. On 9 March, their spring offensive used seven divisions in a limited attack between the Vijose River and Mount Tommorit. The 14 Greek divisions holding the Albanian front gave some ground until the attack was called off on 19 March after heavy casualties on both sides. This remained the position until April 1941 when the German invasion of the Balkans moved through the Pindus, capturing Ioannina, sealing the Greek army in Albania.

Article 3 of the Anglo-Turkish Treaty should have resulted in a Turkish declaration of war against Italy. Arguably the same applied to German troops entering Romania on 7 October, although that was hardly an invasion. However, the British did not even bother to press the point, given the response to earlier requests. The British Ambassador to Greece repeatedly raised the issue but the Foreign Office decided not to do anything.[7] Eden conceded this point in his discussions in Athens on 22 February before the German invasion. He indicated that Turkey would defend her territory but that was all. At the same time, Churchill wanted Middle East Command to seize Italian occupied Rhodes with the British 6th Division, a move that would probably have been welcomed by Turkey. However, the Royal Navy advised it would be unable to protect and supply such an operation.

Hitler was concerned over the Italian invasion and in his letter to Mussolini on 20 November 1940, highlighted the attitude of Turkey, 'because it will have a decisive influence on that of Bulgaria'. As

Greco-Italian War 1940–1941. (Alexikoua, CC BY-SA 4.0)

always, his primary concern was the protection of the Romanian oilfields, which would be within the range of British bombers based in Greece and the islands. He proposed to reach 'some sort of agreement with Turkey in order to relieve Bulgaria from Turkish pressure'. He went on to imply a clear threat to Turkey, 'I am determined, Duce, to oppose with decisive strength any possible attempt by the British to establish a true and real position in Thrace and that at any risk'.

In a later letter (28 February 1941) to Mussolini before the German invasion, he advised that he was writing to İnönü informing him that the entry of German troops into Bulgaria is not directed against Turkey, 'Unless Mr Eden has succeeded in depriving Turkish statesmen and soldiers of their capacity to judge their own interests dispassionately, I see no danger here. In any case, we are of course prepared for anything'. By being 'prepared for anything', Hitler was probably referring to an OKH plan to attack Turkey if it joined the war. The preferred option was an attack after Greek Thrace had been secured. By any standards, this was a quite extraordinary stretch to Operation Marita, although most sources agree that Operation Barbarossa and the invasion of Turkey, were mutually exclusive. In reality, Hitler had little to be concerned about. The Turks had calculated that the British did not have the resources in the region to support Turkey if they joined the conflict and they had little confidence in the other Balkan states.

## Bulgaria

This is a suitable place to consider the position of Turkey's northern neighbour Bulgaria. We have seen that the Italians and Germans understood Bulgaria's concerns, even if they were not convinced it was a real threat. When the Bulgarians again referred to the 37 Turkish divisions in Thrace, Hitler told the Bulgarian Foreign Minister Draganov on 23 November 1940, that the Turks would not attack because they understood the impact of German bombing on Istanbul.[8]

However, from a Bulgarian perspective, the threat was real. When the Italians invaded Greece, Turkey informed Bulgaria that if she attacked Greece, Turkey would declare war. This did help Greece because it allowed them to release divisions from the Bulgarian border to fight in Albania. The Bulgarian-Turkish treaty of friendship was signed on 17 February 1941, which committed both parties not to attack the other. However, neither Germany nor Bulgaria regarded this commitment as a definitive Turkish position, particularly when the Turks had previously indicated that the presence of foreign troops would be a 'hostile act'. Bulgaria was also concerned about the reaction of the Soviet Union. They rejected a Soviet offer to send a military mission in November 1940. If German engagement in Bulgaria became public, there was a concern that the Soviets might seek compensation by seizing the Black Sea port of Varna.

Turkey may not have been an active belligerent until 1945 but it was always considered a threat because it mobilised an army of

German supplied Arado Ar.196 naval reconnaissance floatplane. (Photo by Author, Museum of Aviation and the Air Force, Plovdiv, Bulgaria)

1.3 million men throughout the war. The Turkish First Army (General Altay) deployed at least three corps in Thrace supported by an armoured brigade with over 150 light tanks and a cavalry division. However, even allowing for deployments from other armies, the Bulgarian estimate of 37 divisions was something of an exaggeration. The air force may not have been operationally efficient but it could still deploy over 300 combat aircraft in 1940. These included modern types such as the French M.S 406 and Hawker Hurricanes. The bomber force included American Martin 139Ws, German Heinkel He III and 30 Bristol Blenheims.

Bulgaria had formally declared its neutrality when the war began. However, the incoming government of Bogdan Filov in February 1940 steered the country towards Germany, not least because of hostility towards the Soviet Union. The reward was the cession of Southern Dobruja by Romania on 21 August 1940 under the Treaty of Craiova. They formally joined the Axis on 1 March 1941. The country was in reasonable shape economically, although it lacked a strong industrial base.

In 1938, it adopted a rearmament programme but progress was slow. The air force was supposed to have eight battalions but even this modest force was under strength. Fighter aircraft included 15 PZL P.43B, 15 Avia B-534 and 12 Letov S-328, none of which would be described as modern combat aircraft. The bomber force was slightly better with eight Avia B.71 and 11 Dornier Do17. In

A 105mm field howitzer. Supplied by Germany during the First World War these remained in service throughout the Second World War. (Photo by Author, National Museum of Military History, Sofia)

May 1940, the Bulgarian Air Force became an independent service, which included anti-aircraft defences initially equipped with eight batteries of 20mm guns and four batteries of 88's. In July 1940, the six front-line units (orlaks) were expanded to division (polk) size. The country was also divided into five air fighter zones with squadrons on quick reaction alert. This alert system was strengthened by a German constructed and operated air raid system on the Bulgaria-Greek border. By late 1940, the air force had grown to 305 front-line combat aircraft, including 118 fighters and 67 bombers. These included Messerschmitt Bf 109 E fighters and Do 17 M bombers and larger numbers of ex-Czech Avia fighters.

General Ajanrov commanded the Bulgarian Army, organised in four territorial corps with 10 infantry divisions and 24 frontier

A 75mm D19 M1936 mountain gun. 56 were delivered from Krupp's in 1938 and 40 more arrived in 1940. (Photo by Author, National Museum of Military History, Sofia)

mostly light field guns, with horse-drawn and motorised battalions. Motor vehicles mostly came from Germany, Austria and Czechoslovakia. The infantry truck was mostly the Steyr 440, with Granit 30 reconnaissance cars and Praga and BMW motorcycles.

Bulgaria had very few armoured vehicles. The rapid divisions had Fiat/Ansaldo CV/33 tankettes. In 1936, when Britain was wooing Bulgaria, an agreement was signed on supplying British equipment. This led to the supply of eight Vickers light tanks, of which only four were listed as operational in June 1938.[9] From 1939, Germany became the main military supplier and consumer of Bulgarian goods with a military credit of 45 million Reich Marks. Their priority was tanks for what was called the 'Cover front' with Turkey. This led to the supply of 26 Skoda LT vz.35 tanks by March 1940. Ten further tanks, originally ordered by Afghanistan, were supplied by November 1940. Over 500 Opel Blitz truck chassis were also supplied, with the bodies being manufactured in Bulgaria and artillery tractors and scout cars. Despite this equipment, the Bulgarian Army lagged behind in the modernisation of its army and its transport capacity was barely the same as in the First World War.

The Bulgarian Navy during the Second World War was very small. It consisted of four obsolete Drazki-class torpedo boats, five modern Lurrsen type motor torpedo boats and three former Dutch motor torpedo boats. They cooperated with the Romanian Navy in protecting the Black Sea coast from Soviet raids, with minelaying operations to protect coastal shipping.

Skoda LT vz.35 tank in Bulgarian service. (Photo by Author, National Museum of Military History, Sofia)

battalions. Each division had 15,500 men in three or four three-battalion infantry regiments. Support weapons included an artillery regiment, reconnaissance battalion, machine-gun battalion, engineer battalion, signals and a labour battalion. These divisions were mostly equipped with weapons from the early First World War. Mostly 75mm field guns with a handful of 105mm howitzers and mountain artillery. Anti-tank guns were the 20mm Solothurn, with some more modern Skoda 37mm. There were two rapid divisions, which replaced the cavalry but ended up achieving neither the mobility of cavalry nor the armoured division's punch. They had two cavalry brigades, each with two, five squadron regiments and one, two-battalion motorised infantry regiment. Artillery was again

In the spring of 1940, there were 18 Turkish divisions in Thrace and Gallipoli. The Bulgarian response was the 4th or 'Covering Army' commanding the 4th, 6th and the newly formed 11th Division. The Germans supplied some 75,000 Mannlicher rifles, 3,500 light machine guns, artillery, mortars and anti-tank guns to equip the expansion.[10]

*Drazki*-class torpedo boat. Built at Varna to a French design in 1907 but remained in service throughout the Second World War. (Photo by Kosi Gramatikoff)

## Hitler's Balkan Strategy 1941

The winter of early 1941 had brought a stalemate in the conflicts raging around Turkey. The Italians and Greeks faced off in Albania, while the British had defeated the Italians in Libya. However, with the planned invasion of Britain (Operation Sealion) called off, all of Europe, including Turkey, looked to where Hitler's armies might go next.

The traditional view is that Hitler regarded the Balkans simply as a distraction from his plans to invade the Soviet Union. However, Martin van Creveld suggests a different interpretation.[11] He argues that Hitler was determined on using the Mediterranean as an indirect way of damaging Britain when his invasion plans came to nothing. In October 1940, the German Staffs (General Paulus) even drafted plans for an attack on Egypt through Syria and Iraq via Bulgaria and Turkey,[12] although Hitler rejected the idea because it would bring the Soviets into the picture. It was only when he decided to attack the Soviet Union that his focus changed. Even then, the invasion of Yugoslavia and Greece did not cause any delay to Operation Barbarossa. In this context, van Creveld argues that Hitler gave the green light to Mussolini's invasion of Greece – or at the very least did not impose a veto. In a meeting at the Brenner Pass on 4 October 1940, it seems likely that Hitler accepted that Greece was a matter for Italy while vetoing any invasion of Yugoslavia. The Italian foreign minister, Ciano, said as much to Ribbentrop, who checked with Hitler himself, who did not repudiate this. This also makes sense from a German perspective. It continued the 'war in the periphery' and kept British bombers away from the Romanian oilfields.

German naval planners also favoured a peripheral strategy as an alternative to an invasion of Britain, which they believed could not be achieved without control of the air and sea. In September 1940, Admiral Raeder presented his 'Mediterranean plan' to Hitler, which included a strong German presence in North Africa, capturing Malta, Gibraltar and the Suez Canal. This plan called for an advance through the Middle East to the Turkish border, surrounding Turkey and opening up the Russian oilfields from the south.[13]

Hitler's decision to make a limited intervention in the Balkans was made, in principle, on 4 November 1940, only seven days after Italy had attacked Greece, although implementation would have to be delayed until the spring because of the weather. He was particularly concerned about the Italian failure to attack Crete, which was then occupied by the British. He even offered Mussolini paratroopers for the operation. His plan was part of wider operations in the Mediterranean, including the capture of Gibraltar (vetoed by Franco) and sending Rommel and his Afrika Korps to Libya. Again, his concern was British bombers attacking the Romanian oilfields, as there was a deal brokered with Romania in March 1940 to supply 200,000 tons of oil a month to the Reich. The fanciful schemes of Hitler's engineers to produce synthetic oil had come to nothing, leaving Romania as the main supplier. Hitler told the Soviet foreign minister, Molotov, in November 1940 that he had no political interests in the Balkans. His focus was only on the economic resources essential to the Reich, including the Romanian oilfields.[14]

Special efforts were to be made to reach an agreement with Turkey to relieve Bulgarian concerns. A campaign against Turkey would have been a distraction from the Russian campaign. Hitler was also concerned that the Soviets might incite Turkey against Germany,[15] whilst the Turks were concerned Hitler might sell them out to the Soviets over the Straits. So much so that on 22 November, after the Molotov talks with Hitler added to their concern, Turkey put Thrace under martial law and raised the army alert level. Papen tried to reassure the Turkish leadership the following day but İnönü was not easily convinced.

Hitler also had a growing problem with the Soviet Union's territorial expansion in the Balkans and the failure of attempts at reconciliation. After the meeting with Molotov, he concluded that he would have to invade Russia and that required a safe flank in the Balkans. The Soviets had made clear their interest in Turkey and Bulgaria, as well as Romania and Hungary. Hitler thought he could deal with Yugoslavia diplomatically and only authorised Operation Marita against Greece when his diplomatic overtures there failed. The Italian failure in Albania added to his problems and the coup d'état in Belgrade resulted in a further diversion. However, it also solved logistical difficulties in supplying the 12th Army in Bulgaria

B24 bomber attacking the Romanian oilfields at Ploesti. Romania was the biggest producer of oil in Europe during the Second World War and protecting German interests in this was a key consideration in Hitler's Balkan strategy. (44th Bomb Group Photograph Collection)

and made it easier to manoeuvre the panzer divisions around the Greek positions by going through southern Yugoslavia.

When German troops entered Bulgaria, Turkey closed the Dardanelles. Churchill wrote to İnönü in January offering anti-aircraft guns and sought permission to base 100 RAF squadrons in Turkey, although where these aircraft would come from is unclear. Hitler wrote to the Turkish President on 4 March 1941, emphasising his peaceful intentions towards Turkey and guaranteeing that German troops would stay at least 35miles from the border. Turkey's less than aggressive response reassured Hitler and he even contemplated giving Turkey a strip of Greek territory around Edirne. The British had access to intercepted Italian and Japanese communications, which indicated that the Axis had few concerns over a new Balkan front on the Turkish border.

### Operation Marita and Yugoslavia

A German attack on Greece was a significant logistical challenge, regardless of the diplomatic difficulties. Troops and equipment would have to come from Germany, Austria and Poland, through Hungary and into Romania along railway lines with limited capacity. There the problems would really start as there were no bridges over the Danube so it required temporary bridges, difficult to achieve secretly. Once in Bulgaria, the troops would face a march of several hundred miles before reaching the Greek border. There was only one railway line from Bulgaria to Salonika, other than a line that ran too close to the Turkish border. The Greek border was defended by the Metaxas Line, a series of modern fortifications built between 1936 and 1939.

If German troops could use Yugoslavian rail lines to Bulgaria, the journey could be almost halved. Yugoslavia also controlled the two best road links into Greece through the Monastir Gap and the Vardar Valley. German diplomacy turned to Yugoslavia ruled by Prince Paul, Regent for the young King Peter. Diplomatic pressure from Germany was nothing new for the British educated prince. In June 1939, he made a state visit to Germany and resisted efforts to join the Axis. Hitler, in a moment of pique, suggested to Mussolini that Italy should invade Yugoslavia. This almost irresistible temptation had to be turned down because Mussolini was unprepared for a war that August.

Yugoslavia was also ill-prepared for war. The country lacked defensible natural borders and was surrounded by countries with their own territorial claims on it. It had a limited industrial base and was politically divided, particularly between Serbia and Croatia. The 'Serbianisation' of the military meant the General Staff was 90 percent Serb, with only a handful of Croat or Slovene general officers. This had been exploited by Mussolini for many years, encouraging the Croat nationalist leader Pavelic. The Royal Yugoslav Army (VKJ) on paper had 1.4 million men in 34 divisions and other units,[16] although few would reach full strength when the Germans invaded. Mechanisation was limited and only a handful of modern weapons existed, including two battalions of Renault R35 tanks and Czech artillery and anti-tank guns. The air force (JKRV) had over 420 aircraft, including 100 modern fighters and 100 modern bombers. The navy (KJRM) had 27 ships and four submarines, supported by 120 aircraft. However, this was hopelessly inadequate to defend the long Adriatic coastline.

After the outbreak of war in September 1939, we have already seen that Paul discussed with the French and the British the possibility of an Allied landing at Salonika. Salonika was crucial to Yugoslavia as her only outlet to the sea outside the Adriatic, once Albania was in Italian hands. Paul even sought a rapprochement with the Soviet Union when the British could not supply weapons and equipment. Yugoslavia did provide the Greeks with horses and other materials during their conflict with Italy. They also blocked German attempts to supply the Italians through Yugoslavia.

British strategy focused on creating a Balkan bloc against Germany composed of Turkey, Greece, Yugoslavia and Bulgaria. Greece had to be defended because German access to ports in the Aegean would threaten the Middle East. Turkey needed support to resist a German thrust through Turkey to the Middle East and because she had large armed forces. British attempts to get negotiations started between Yugoslavia and Turkey faced significant barriers. They took the Turkish initiative for conversations at face value, while the Yugoslavs were not so trusting.[17] The Turkish-Bulgaria non-aggression pact of 17 February 1941 did not inspire confidence, confirming that the Turks were clearly not prepared to take any risks on behalf of Yugoslavia. The Soviets also opened negotiations with Yugoslavia, although this was always going to fall short of a military alliance, which would have been a serious provocation to the Germans, something Stalin was desperate to avoid. He did hope that the Yugoslavs would put up a stiff defence, which would mean the Germans would have to postpone any attack on the Soviet Union until the next spring.

Royal Yugoslav Army, Bofors 150mm M31 Howitzer. (Photo by Author, Belgrade Kalemegdan)

Rupel Pass on the Greece-Bulgaria border. The German 5th Mountain Division was initially repulsed here by Greek troops defending the Metaxas Line. (Photo by Author)

This all leads to the fateful events of March 1941. Hitler effectively gave Prince Paul an ultimatum to support the Axis or face invasion. The British urged him to fight without promising any practical support. British intervention in Greece was inadequate to save the Greeks, let alone supply and equip the hopelessly divided Yugoslavian armed forces. The Crown Council concluded that there was no option other than joining the Axis and Prince Paul assented. He believed he was doing so under conditions that would have protected Yugoslavia. However, he was inevitably regarded as a traitor to the Allied cause, a view that dogged him for the rest of his life. This sparked a long-planned coup d'état by Serbian officers, which used King Peter, who was just short of his 18th birthday, as cover. Prince Paul made no real effort to resist the coup and was probably relieved to leave the country.

Hitler was furious, drawing on his Austrian hatred of Serbia from the times of the Austro-Hungarian Empire. The Soviet non-aggression pact with Yugoslavia did not deter him, declaring that without action, the Balkans could be lost, including Turkey. He responded by ordering an invasion of Yugoslavia (Directive 25, 27 March 1941). With remarkable speed, the plan was executed on 6 April, starting with a massive air attack on Belgrade and airfields across the country. The German Second Army attacked from Austria, driving through Croatia towards Belgrade, while the First Panzer Group attacked from Bulgaria into the south of the

British propaganda view of the strategic situation in April 1941. (Author's Collection, *War Illustrated*, 4 April 1941)

country. Subordinate attacks were made from Romania, Hungary and Italy. The two main German prongs cut through VKJ units on both fronts (German troops were cheered on entering Zagreb) and Belgrade surrendered on 12 April. They then combined to destroy the remnants of the Yugoslav forces before an armistice was signed on 17 April. German casualties in 12 days of combat, totalled only 558 men.

The collapse of Yugoslavia allowed XL Panzer Corps to push into Greece from Yugoslavia. The Greek army was concentrated in Albania and along the Metaxas Line facing Bulgaria, leaving weaker forces to face the German attack. They refused to make strategic withdrawals proposed by the British to create a realistic defensive line. 2nd Panzer Division cut through the Greek 19th Mechanised Division and captured Salonika on 10 April. The Metaxas Line held out heroically for several days against German mountain divisions, before they broke through, capturing western Thrace.

The British had sent an expeditionary force to Greece known as W Force (General Wilson) consisting of the 6th Australian Division, 2nd New Zealand Division and the British 1st Armoured Brigade, with support units and air cover. The Greeks (Papagos had taken over as prime minister after Metaxas' death on 19 January) wanted 10 divisions but accepted the forces allocated. Wavell was initially opposed to the expedition (Operation Lustre), which diverted scarce resources from the Middle East. He even doubted the Germans would invade but Churchill had seen the Enigma decrypts and was convinced it was not a bluff. Eden had an optimistic view of the prospects of getting Turkey engaged and this, along with political commitments to Greece, may have changed his mind when he cabled his support to Churchill from the region.[18] In contrast, whatever the strategic position of Turkey, Wavell believed the Turks were too weak to be of much use militarily without more armour and aircraft. However, he changed his mind on Greece accepting

German War Cemetery overlooking Maleme Airfield, Crete. The Fallschirmjäger casualties were so high that Hitler was reluctant to authorise large scale airborne operations during the rest of the war. (Photo by Author)

Allied memorial at the small village of Sfakia on the south coast of Crete where more than 6,000 troops evacuated on 29–30 May 1941. (Photo by Author)

division in reserve at Plovdiv, just in case of a Turkish attack.

The British plan was to defend the Aliakmon Line, which stretched from Mount Olympus through the Vermion Range to the Yugoslav border. That line became unhinged when the German XL Panzer Corps came through the Monastir Gap, exposing the flank of the Greek First Army, which was eventually cut off and surrendered on 23 April. Meanwhile, the British had withdrawn to the Thermopylae line as the first stage in the agreed withdrawal from Greece with the Greek government. Nearly 14,000 Allied troops were taken prisoner and a further 903 were killed and 1250 wounded. The Greek Navy suffered heavily during the campaign, losing 12 destroyers and an old battleship. One old cruiser, two destroyers and eight torpedo boats escaped. By the end of the war, the large Greek merchant marine lost 75 percent of its tonnage.

Taking a quick look at this campaign, it looks like another triumph for Blitzkrieg. In practice, it was not, with the Germans losing a lot of armour as they struggled to fight their way through the mountain passes of Greece. The British and Commonwealth troops made effective use of anti-tank guns and demolitions to slow progress and their mobility and flexibility were impressive. This is confirmed by German views of the campaign.[19]

the political considerations over the military ones saying, 'war is an option of difficulties'. Churchill again lurched from supporting action in Greece to abandoning the mainland in return for a defensive position in the Dodecanese or a further offensive in Libya. The debate ended when the War Cabinet felt they had no option other than to honour its commitments to Greece.

Not that it had any effect on the Turks. Eden and General Dill had visited Ankara in March but they were told Turkey would defend itself only if attacked. Eden even proposed a political declaration of war against Germany without any military action. The Turks understandably found this proposal incredulous. Churchill's rhetoric lurched from accusing Turkey of shirking their responsibilities to exclaiming the benefits of armed neutrality. Bulgaria did not directly participate in the attack on Greece and moved its armies to the border with Turkey and Greece. The Germans kept a panzer

The German 164th Division secured the Aegean coast up to the Turkish border and seized the islands with support from airborne units and the 6th Mountain Division. Crete was attacked (Operation Mercury) and was evacuated by 1 June. The campaign also enabled Rommel to attack the weakened Allied forces in Libya, resulting in the loss of the early war gains in that theatre. By splitting their forces, the British achieved neither objective and Wavell, never a Churchill favourite was moved on.

As Bulgaria now had secure northern and western borders, most of its army shifted to the east coast and the Turkish border in Thrace. Bulgarian troops occupied Morava and Macedonia with the newly formed 5th Army, including the 6th and 7th Infantry divisions and the 1st Rapid Division. The 2nd Army took West Thrace up to the Turkish border including, 10th Infantry Division, 2nd Border Brigade and 1st Infantry Replacement Regiment. In June 1941,

British propaganda promoted a very positive view of the preparedness of the Turkish armed forces after Operation Marita. (Author's Collection, *War Illustrated*, 4 April 1941)

it may rank with the finest military establishments of the continent'. In terms of later events in 1941, a comparison with Japan might have been viewed in the editorial office as somewhat unfortunate.[21] In reality, the British military assessment was that Turkey could not defend Thrace against a German attack, with German forces reaching the Straits in six weeks. However, they were more sanguine about defending Anatolia and pointed to the number of troops the Germans would require to defend their lines of communication to the Middle East. We have limited insight into German thinking at the time but it seems that they had a similar assessment.

### War at Sea

The war at sea in the eastern Mediterranean also stepped up a gear in 1940. Naval warfare has historically been crucial to controlling the Mediterranean and to commerce. In 1938, 86 percent of Italy's imports arrived by sea and most of that came through British controlled chokepoints at Gibraltar and Suez. Convoy protection played a key role for the Italian and British fleets. In Britain's case, to reinforce Malta and its armies in North Africa and for Italy, the shorter crossing to Tunis and Tripoli. More surface actions were fought in the Mediterranean by more participants than anywhere else in the war. A total of 55, compared with 49 in the Atlantic and 36 in the Pacific.

The Italian Navy was much larger than the British Mediterranean fleet commanded by Admiral Cunningham now that the French fleet was out of the war. The Italians had four older and two modern battleships, seven heavy and 12 light cruisers. In addition, they had about 60 destroyers, 120 submarines and numerous motor torpedo boats. They also had innovative assault boats loaded with explosives and piloted torpedoes, to penetrate enemy ports and attack shipping. The Italian Navy was technically competent, including gunnery, communication and manoeuvres. It is a well-worn myth that the Italian Navy was useless.[22] In fact, it fought hard and well, keeping Italy's African and Balkan armies supplied for three years and largely controlling the central Mediterranean.

In Rome, the Japanese naval attaché reported that the Italian Navy was sound; their problems were poor collaboration with the

the Aegean Sea Detachment (*Belomorski Otryad*) was created for occupation duties which included two infantry regiments, the Aegean Fleet, two labour battalions and support units. In January 1942, Bulgaria also occupied the Morava Valley region in Serbia using the 6th, 17th and 21st Infantry Divisions (I Corps). This freed up more German units for the eastern front and was extended to more occupation tasks in 1942, which drew Bulgaria into the developing anti-Partisan war. The German focus was on plunder. German *Sonderkommando* units looted antiquities, searched for Jews and seized anything of economic value.

Turkey was taking no chances and moved more units into Thrace. British propaganda over the strength of the Turkish army went into overdrive. The April 1941 edition of *War Illustrated* gave an overview of the Turkish military and the delivery of new equipment.[20] It went so far as to say, 'in some very important respects

Air Force and outdated night-fighting techniques. Their submarine fleet, although large, were less deadly than their German counterparts due to unrealistic training and flawed doctrine. The absence of aircraft carriers and radar put the fleet at a disadvantage away from the coast and their anti-submarine detection systems were basic. Throughout the war, the Italian fleet was constrained by limited fuel supplies. This has been presented as an excuse for inactivity but the lack of bunker fuel was confirmed by an objective witness, the German Admiral Weichold.[23]

The Fairey Swordfish was the Royal Navy's main torpedo bomber in the Mediterranean. Their attack at Taranto resulted in the Italian fleet losing half of its capital ships in one night. (Photo by Tony Hisgett)

In the best tradition of the Royal Navy, the size of the Italian fleet did not stop Cunningham from taking an aggressive posture, sailing his whole fleet to prod the Italians into a fleet action. At this stage of the war, the impact of airpower on naval warfare was not fully appreciated. Even Churchill, who was usually quick to support innovation, had declared in 1938 that anti-aircraft armament would enable even a single armed vessel to hold its own against aircraft. The British only had one aircraft carrier (HMS *Eagle*) in the Mediterranean and the few RAF maritime reconnaissance aircraft were not trained to operate with the fleet.[24]

The new carrier HMS *Illustrious* also allowed Cunningham to launch an audacious air attack on the main Italian naval base at Taranto, seriously damaging three Italian battleships. The Royal Navy had some important advantages against the Italians. Not least their better intelligence, having cracked the Italian and German codes but also the use of radar on ships. This meant they knew roughly when and where convoys were going. The British also excelled at night fighting, which meant they could engage without being interdicted from the air. The Royal Navy only lost three major warships, all destroyers, due to Italian surface action throughout the war.

With Axis convoys to North Africa being threatened, the Luftwaffe's X Fliegerkorps with 330 aircraft, was deployed to Italy. The Ju 87 crews had been trained in naval dive-bombing techniques and they quickly had an impact, damaging the *Illustrious*. This forced the British into defensive measures, including more fighter aircraft and better anti-aircraft gunnery. The fleet was heavily involved in defending the convoys taking troops to Greece and the Italians sortied out to attack them. At the Battle of Cape Matapan (27–29 March 1941), the Italians lost three cruisers, two destroyers and others, including the battleship *Vittorio Veneto*, were damaged. It was Italy's greatest defeat at sea and severely limited their operations for the rest of the war.

**Operation Barbarossa**

Although Turkey and the Allies did not know it, Hitler's 'peripheral' strategy effectively came to an end in November 1940 due to deteriorating relations with the Soviet Union. Stalin's price for a new deal was more than Hitler was prepared to pay, particularly in the Balkans. This is confirmed by the recollections of OKW chiefs Keitel and Jodl, who confirmed that Soviet penetration into Romania was one of Hitler's primary concerns. The mutual assistance pact between the Soviet Union and Bulgaria and a long-term lease on land and naval bases within range of the Bosporus and Dardanelles, added to his concerns. While Germany would have to prop up the Italians, the strategy in the eastern Mediterranean would be essentially defensive. Barbarossa is often portrayed as the inevitable consequence of Hitler's ideology as set out in *Mein Kampf*. Even if this is the case, the timing of Barbarossa is linked to his clash with Stalin over the Balkans. If Britain's refusal to reach a peace agreement was because they hoped to inveigle the Soviets into the war, then that could be stopped by crushing the Soviet Union in a short war. The objectives were never total occupation but rather the limited objectives of capturing valuable economic regions in the south of Russia.

The study of the decision to launch Operation Barbarossa has traditionally focused on German-Soviet relationships since the Molotov-Ribbentrop Pact of 1939. As Gabriel Gorodetsky shows in his study based on Soviet and German archives,[25] historians have missed the equally important relationships with Britain, Turkey and the Balkan states. Stalin had a long-standing hostility towards Britain, going back to the British intervention during the Russian Civil War when they executed 26 commissars in Baku. However, it was the threat of British naval intervention through the Straits and into the Black Sea that concerned him at the outbreak of the Second World War. His historical timeline referenced the Crimean War and support for White armies in the Crimea and Odessa in 1918 and 1919. His first action on the outbreak of war was to offer military assistance to Turkey to help secure the Straits. Stalin feared Britain more than he did Germany. The 1939 mutual assistance treaty between Turkey and Britain reinforced his concerns, as did the disclosure of the British/French plan to bomb the Baku oilfields.

The Germans understood this fear and played on it to justify their own initiatives in the Balkans. They even explained their invasion of Norway as blocking British support for Finland in their war against the Soviet Union. The Italians also reached an understanding with the Soviets, which gave them a free hand in the Mediterranean while the Soviet Union controlled the Black Sea. Stalin understood the Axis need for Romanian oil and he saw the occupation of Bessarabia as a trade-off that gave him some protection against any thrust into Ukraine from the Balkans. In particular, the occupation of Northern Bukovina left the Soviets in control of the railway lines between Bessarabia and Ukraine. However, in 1940, the primary concern was to control the Danube egress into the Black Sea, which the Soviets regarded as an inland sea.

Attempts by the British to portray German moves in the Balkans as a threat to the Soviet Union were viewed by Stalin as an attempt to get them to fight Germany on Britain's behalf. He also did not rule out the British seeking a separate peace with Germany as the French had done. The flight of Hitler's deputy, Rudolph Hess, to Britain in May 1941 is regarded in Britain as the action of a deranged individual. In contrast, it fed Stalin's concern of a separate peace, a point he persisted with in exchanges as late as 1944. British records reveal that the Foreign Office did manipulate the affair in order to disrupt German-Soviet negotiations in 1941,[26] which may have had the unforeseen consequences of adding to Stalin's interpretation.

Hitler's focus was now on Operation Barbarossa (Directive 21), which was agreed on 18 December 1940. Some 3.8 million Axis troops were to be deployed for the invasion across a broad front in June 1941. However, Bulgaria would not be declaring war on the Soviet Union, so no part of the offensive would start near Turkish territory. Soviet intelligence was not asleep in the run-up to the invasion. Regular reports were submitted on the German troop build-up and Soviet spies confirmed the likelihood of an attack. However, these were presented by Soviet agencies in the context of Stalin's view that war was not inevitable. Churchill's description of Stalin as a 'simpleton' is contradicted by British records and Cabinet discussions, which show that the information was not as definitive as Churchill later claimed in his memoirs.[27] As we have seen, Britain's warning would be viewed sceptically anyway, as the British Ambassador to Moscow frequently pointed out to London. Stalin was desperate to avoid war for another year at least, to give time for the Red Army to make ready. He was, therefore, prepared to go the extra mile in negotiations.

Historians have debated at length if Operation Marita delayed Operation Barbarossa, possibly fatally given that the offensive ground to a halt in the snow before Moscow. The modern view is that it did not. Only a handful of divisions deployed in Marita were scheduled for front-line action in Barbarossa, most being in the OKW reserves. The unusually wet winter kept the rivers in full flood until late spring and there was still plenty of time to reach Moscow before winter. Many logistical and other preparations went slower than planned, which did not involve units deployed in the Balkans. It could even be argued that Marita camouflaged Barbarossa from the Soviets.

The invasion of the Soviet Union caused a sigh of relief in Turkey, although they probably had more than a suspicion it was coming given the approaches of von Papen. When he heard the news, the Turkish Foreign Minister Saracoğlu was reported to have jumped on stage at a Tavern in Ankara and danced until dawn. However, that was quickly followed by a concern that Britain would become too close to the Soviet Union. Churchill's view is summed up in his statement, 'If Hitler invaded Hell, I would make at least a favourable reference to the Devil in the House of Commons'. However, in a speech on 22 June, he went further, saying that Russia had been hard done by in the First World War. Not for the first time, Churchillian rhetoric kept the Foreign Office busy playing down the comments to the Turks who remembered Russian war aims included the Straits. The Germans played on these fears by releasing 1940 Soviet proposals for bases on the Straits, arguing that only Hitler could stop the advance of Bolshevism.

Turkey had survived the Axis occupation of the Balkans with its territorial integrity intact by taking a pragmatic view of the military reality. They had played the diplomatic cards of possible alliances with the Soviets to discourage them from military action, while such moves were also aimed at discouraging the Germans. Britain's naive

Mehmet Şükrü Saracoğlu the Turkish Minister of Foreign Affairs during the early stages of the Second World War. He signed the German-Turkish Treaty of Friendship in 1941. (Albert Grandolini Collection)

view that Turkey would be a leader in the Balkans also ended in the face of reality in 1941. However, Turkey was not protected by any exceptional judgement or diplomatic genius; in the end it was Hitler's failed invasion of the Soviet Union that protected Turkey.

## Operation Abstention and the Aegean

In February 1941, the British, flushed with the successful raid on the Italian fleet at Taranto, decided to strengthen their position in the Aegean by capturing the Italian held island of Castelorizzo. The island is the easternmost of the Dodecanese Islands, 80 miles from Rhodes and just off the Turkish coast. The aim was to develop the existing motor torpedo base to threaten Italian positions in the islands.

The attack was launched on 25 February by 50 Commando who surprised the small Italian garrison and Royal Marines captured the harbour. The Italians counterattacked from Rhodes by air and the next day, landed troops on the island as the Italian Navy disrupted British attempts to reinforce the island. They were demonstrating again that the Italian Navy was a force to be reckoned with. On 28 February, reinforcements from the Sherwood Foresters were landed on the island but the commander quickly concluded that without air or naval support, the operation was unsustainable. The bulk of the British troops re-embarked but a number of commandos were left behind and captured.[28]

Admiral Cunningham described the operation as 'a rotten business and reflected little credit to everyone'. Churchill wrote that he was 'thoroughly mystified'. The lessons learned report highlighted that Italian morale was not as low as planners had assumed.[29] Capturing an island is relatively easy but defending it against counterattack from an enemy force based nearby is an altogether different prospect. They recommended that 'we should not attempt to use islands upon which our garrisons cannot be supported by fighter aircraft and light naval forces'. Sadly, as we will see, lessons that were again ignored in 1943.

Unsurprisingly, this episode did little to reassure the Turks that Britain was in a position to retake the Dodecanese islands for them. Further operations, including a planned attack on Kasos (Operation

Typical caique sailed by the Levant Schooner Flotilla in the Aegean. (Adrian Seligman, Public Domain)

operated observation positions on remote islands. The Greek Sacred Squadron grew from 140 to 350 men commanded by Colonel Tsigantes. They took an increasing role in raiding operations as the war progressed. The Levant Schooner Flotilla (LSF),[30] commanded by Lt Cdr Adrian Seligman, used small boats known as caiques to infiltrate agents and supplies to partisans. Mostly sailing boats, they were often motorised using obsolete Matilda tank engines and armed with captured Italian weapons. They often flew Greek or Turkish flags, a legitimate naval ruse de guerre, so long as they are hauled down before opening fire.

Blunt) and a much broader attack on Rhodes and the other islands (Operation Mandibles), were cancelled.

Practical action in the Aegean was limited to special forces grouped under the command of Brigadier Turnbull in GHQ Middle East Command. These included the Special Boat Squadron (SBS) commanded by Major, the Earl Jellico, son of the British fleet commander at Jutland. They specialised in raiding from the sea. The Long Range Desert Group (LRDG) was formed to carry out reconnaissance behind enemy lines and when the desert war came to an end, they were allocated to raiding operations in the Aegean. By August 1943, they had grown to 10 patrols of 15 to 18 men who

One unit we know little about was the Kalpaks, known unofficially as the enthusiastic (Kurdish) thugs. This unit consisted of a British officer and 19 other ranks whose nationality is unclear. If they were Kurds, the Turks would not have been happy. The original aim was to infiltrate them into the Caucasus to assassinate German generals but they ended the war in the Aegean.

All of these units engaged in a wide range of operations in the Aegean.[31] These included raiding airfields on Crete and Rhodes with mixed success. Raids on the smaller islands did force the Germans to strengthen island garrisons and played an important role in deception operations later in the war.

# 6
# ENCIRCLEMENT 1941–1942

By the summer of 1941, Turkey was surrounded by Axis forces, with the doubtful exception of its border with the Soviet Union. Even that might be endangered as the panzers rolled towards the Crimea and the Caucasus.

The Turkish army responded by concentrating its forces to defend Thrace from the Bulgarians in the north and the Germans, Bulgarians and Italians in Greece and the islands.[1] The First Army (General Altay), headquartered in Istanbul, deployed three corps in Thrace. X Corps, which included the armoured brigade, at Kirklareli. XX Corps and IV Corps with four infantry divisions each in the Çatalca defences. Finally, III Corps with four infantry divisions at Corlu. The Second Army (General Gurman) was based in the Dardanelles and Marmara area. II Corps defended Gallipoli on the European side of the Straits with four infantry divisions. I Corps was opposite at Çanakkale and V Corps further back at Bursa. XII Corps, with three infantry divisions and other units, defended the Aegean and Mediterranean coasts based at Izmir. The VI Corps (three divisions) was held as a General Staff reserve on the Sea of Marmara at Izmit. The remainder of the Turkish army was deployed near the border with the Soviet Union with the Third Army (12 divisions) based at Erzincan and XVII Corps (three divisions) covering the Syrian border from Maras.

These deployments came with civil preparations to evacuate the population of Istanbul to Anatolia, along with blackouts and improved anti-aircraft defences, including over 100 anti-aircraft guns. The air force had grown to 500 aircraft deployed in 11 (two squadron) battalions. Additional classes were also drafted into the army, although many were deployed in road construction rather than military training. In total, the army had expanded from 11 to 17 corps with 43 infantry, two cavalry and two mechanised divisions.

British efforts to engage Turkey in the war, albeit defensively during this period, became more important as events in the Middle East highlighted the risks of Turkey becoming an Axis back door to Allied interests. Events in Iraq, Syria and specifically Iran emphasised Turkish concerns about the Soviets expanding along their eastern borders. This, coupled with Allied weakness, pushed Turkey into its most pro-German period of the war.

Turkish army deployment in Thrace. (Author)

### German Approaches to Turkey

While the British had not given up on enticing Turkey into the war, the Germans saw their military victories as an opportunity to bring them over to the Axis. Turkey also recognised that they would need to come to terms with the Axis and negotiations began.

Ribbentrop wanted unlimited transit rights, although Papen advised that the Turks would do nothing that pointed towards Britain and some minor territorial revisions would not change that position. These revisions focused on Aleppo in Syria, Mosul in Iraq and some of the Greek islands. The Turks even kept the British advised of the progress of talks, justifying them by referencing their strategic isolation. Turkey used her military deployments in negotiations with the Germans while emphasising their inability to resist to the British.

The Turkish-German Treaty of Friendship and Non-Aggression was signed on 18 June 1941. It had no significant military obligations but from a German perspective it neutralised Turkey on the eve of Operation Barbarossa. The official media line was that the treaty meant Turkey was allied to Britain and friends with Germany.[2] In practice, it was more a propaganda gain for the Germans and reflected British weakness following military defeats in the Balkans and North Africa. It also built upon long-standing economic ties between Germany and Turkey, with as many as 50 German firms operating in Turkey. German banks even sold looted gold in Turkey to finance their espionage and propaganda activities.[3]

It was followed in October 1941 by the Clodius Agreement. Turkey agreed to export up 45,000 tons of chromite ore to Germany in 1941–1942 and 90,000 tons of the mineral in each of 1943 and 1944, contingent on Germany's supplies of military equipment to Turkey. The Germans provided as many as 117 railway locomotives and 1,250 freight rail cars to transport the ore. This still honoured agreements with Britain, so it actually fell short of what the

Exchange of the ratification documents for the German-Turkish Friendship Treaty 1941. From left to right, the Deputy Secretary General in the Turkish Foreign Ministry, Ambassador Acikalin, the Turkish Ambassador in Berlin R. Hüsrev Gerede and State Secretary V. Weizsäcker from the German Foreign Office. (Bundesarchiv Bild 183-B03617)

Focke-Wulf Fw 190A, similar to those supplied to Turkey. (USAAF)

Germans wanted. They swallowed the deal, given that Turkey was their major source of the mineral.

The deal also brought advanced German military equipment. Negotiations that started in October 1941 led to the supply of 72 Focke-Wulf Fw-190A-3 fighter aircraft beginning in July 1942. They were deployed initially at Eskisehir in central Anatolia. This was an astonishing sale of advanced fighter aircraft given the growing pressure on German industrial production from Allied bombing. However, by the end of the war, spare parts were unobtainable, so operational capability was limited. They were buried after the war at Kayseri and after a long struggle, some are now restored in the aviation museum.[4]

### Iraq and Syria

After the First World War, Iraq became a country carved out of the former Ottoman territories around Basra, Baghdad and Mosul. The British and French had carved up this part of the Middle East in the Sykes-Picot agreement in 1918, the infamous 'line in the sand',[5] France taking Syria and the British taking Palestine, Transjordan and Iraq.

Britain had found Iraq ungovernable with frequent revolts and it became a financial burden greater than the benefits of an air bridge to India justified. The solution was indirect rule, with a new ruling dynasty, led by King Feisal, installed after massive vote-rigging. Iraq would have its own army supported by the RAF, which had become adept at low-cost colonial policing. The country formally became independent in 1932 but the British retained a degree of control and two air bases – Habbaniya, near Baghdad and Shaiba, near Basra. This arrangement did not resolve internal conflicts between the Sunni minority and the Shia majority, not to mention the Kurds in the north or the scattering of other communities. There were also endemic conflicts between the tribes and the cities, landowners and peasants and political differences between Iraq nationalists and pan-Arabists in a non-functioning democracy. If this all sounds familiar to the modern reader, nothing much has changed.

The French had had similar problems in Syria. After expelling the Arab leadership in 1922, they faced a major insurrection by the Druse between 1925 and 1927. The French had promised independence but after the fall of France in 1940, Syria came under the control of Vichy France. Turkey had settled its border issues with France in Syria but had the oilfields of Mosul in northern Iraq in its sights. To strengthen their position, they moved troops up to the Syria and Iraq borders. The Iraqis were anti-British but also opposed Turkish imperialism. In addition, they had a reasonably modern army of four infantry divisions and 60 combat aircraft.

On 1 April 1941, the Golden Square coup was launched by four Iraqi colonels, which overthrew the Regent and installed Rashid Ali al-Gaylani as Prime Minister. The Golden Square was mildly fascist, a home-grown version rather than being overtly pro-Axis. They approached the Germans for support, who sent a small number of aircraft along with Italian fighters. Vichy Syria assisted with logistics, including airfields for staging and refuelling. Wavell was not keen to get involved militarily. He pointed to the lack of guns and tanks in Palestine and how stretched his forces were. He suggested diplomatic action by Turkey or the USA was a better option. This suggestion did not go down well at the Foreign Office and raised Churchill's blood pressure considerably.[6] He was ordered to take specific action and Britain responded by sending the 20th Indian Infantry Brigade to occupy Basra. Iraq forces besieged the RAF airfield at Habbaniya but British air superiority forced them back to Fallujah. The airfield was relieved by the Habforce and Kingcol columns, who crossed the desert from Palestine and Transjordan. The British then advanced on Baghdad, which fell on 31 May and the Regent returned to power.

The coup plotters had overestimated their internal and external support. The Germans had assumed the Iraq army was strong enough to contain the British and provided inadequate forces to support the coup. As Barrie James concludes,[7] the Germans could have taken Iraq for a modest investment of military resources. The British had responded brilliantly with meagre resources, given the loss of Iraq would have had disastrous consequences across the Middle East. German armoured forces in Iraq and Syria would have undermined the defence of Egypt, although such forces would have needed rail access through Turkey. It was this that drove the British to pursue a strong military rather than a diplomatic solution to the Iraq crisis and demonstrate to the Turks that they were in a position to stop the Axis encirclement of Turkey.

Interestingly, the USA was not unsympathetic towards Rashid Ali. They believed that without his neutrality, Turkey would have seized Iraq and gone on to regain other parts of the Ottoman Empire. This reflected Rashid Ali's concern that Turkey and Germany would reach an agreement to carve up Iraq. It seems clear that the Turkish leadership did briefly flirt with the idea of a more comprehensive pact with Germany over the Iraq revolt.[8] The Turkish Foreign Minister collaborated over the text of a draft treaty but the President eventually decided to return to their policy of strict neutrality and the weaker subsequent treaty.

Turkish and British troops meet on the Syrian border. (Albert Grandolini Collection)

The Iraq revolt also brought a new player to the game, Imperial Japan. The Tripartite Pact had not clearly defined spheres of influence and the Japanese were taking the view that Asia extended far enough to include the Middle East to reflect their economic interests in the region. They had partly financed the coup and promised military supplies. The Germans would not cooperate with Japanese plans and not wanting to upset the Japanese may have been a factor in German and Turkish response to the coup. The British also took this seriously. Turkish reports indicated that Eden was expecting Japanese landings in Aden, which he was doubtful the British could resist.

During the Iraq campaign, the RAF had attacked Syrian airfields. On 8 June, British and Empire forces attacked Syria (Operation Exporter) with around 34,000 men in four columns from Palestine and Iraq. These included the 7th Australian Division, 1st Free French Division, 10th Indian Infantry Division and two other Indian brigades with support units. The Vichy French defenders had 35,000 troops and 90 tanks. Most of the Vichy air force was destroyed on the ground, which was just as well as they heavily outnumbered the RAF. However, land forces resisted the Allied advance, with fierce fighting in several places. This was anything but the walk-in that Churchill had expected when he forced this operation on Wavell. Nevertheless, after weeks of hard fighting, as the Australian 21st Brigade approached Beirut, the Vichy commander sought an armistice, which came into effect on 12 July.

The conflict could have expanded dramatically if a scheme proposed by Admiral Darlan been agreed. He proposed reinforcing the Vichy French army with four battalions from France escorted by the battleship Strasbourg, four cruisers and a division of destroyers. The British, through signals intelligence, were alerted and even the Germans were surprised at France's willingness to engage in a fleet action with the British.[9] In the end, nothing happened, probably because the loss of the French fleet would have squandered their best asset.

While the Syrian campaign was eventually a much-needed success, the resources deployed largely came from the desert offensive against Rommel. Operation Battleaxe failed and gave Churchill the excuse he was looking for to replace Wavell. He also poured reinforcements into Egypt at the expense of the Far East, which would have consequences later in the year.

For Turkey, the Syrian campaign brought the war very close to their recently acquired province of Hatay and other parts of the border. They moved troops to that border and made it clear that they would not tolerate incursions. The British even briefly considered allowing the Turks to occupy Aleppo, although given the recent treaty with Germany, it was unlikely that the Turks would take the risk. Wavell was equally concerned about supplies reaching Vichy Syria through Turkey. He ordered Bill Slim (later to command in Burma) and his 10th Indian Division to head for Aleppo, cutting off the rail link. The Turks also noted that the Germans did not seriously intervene in Syria. Hitler was focused elsewhere and felt Crete was already too exposed.

### Iran

In many ways, more worrying for the Turkish leadership, was the British-Soviet invasion (Operation Countenance) of Iran on 25 August 1941. Iran was ruled by Reza Shah, who was slowly modernising the country with help from the Germans and others. Germany appealed to Iran as a partner because it lacked a history of imperialism in the region. Relations with Britain were strained since Iran rescinded the Anglo-Iranian Oil Company's exclusive right to sell Iranian oil. The Abadan oil refinery produced 8 million tons of oil in 1940. Axis support for the Iraq revolt confirmed British worries that Germany might seek to control Iranian oil. In addition, following Operation Barbarossa, the Soviet Union was now a British ally and the Trans-Iranian Railway was the easiest way to supply the Soviet Union with Lend-Lease equipment from the USA. The Allies, therefore, increased the pressure on Iran to expel Germans from the country. To preserve their neutrality, some German trade was reduced but Germans continued to hold important positions in strategic industries.

Soviet tankmen of the 6th Tank Division drive through the streets of Tabriz. (Albert Grandolini Collection)

The Iranian army had made efforts to modernise but these were not completed by the outbreak of war. The army consisted of 120,000 to 200,000 men in nine infantry divisions. The 1st and 2nd Divisions had 100 FT6 and Panzer 38(t) light tanks and LaFrance TK-6 armoured cars.

The British assembled a naval task force to capture the key ports of Khuzestan in the Persian Gulf, where the best Iranian divisions were stationed. A naval bombardment followed by troop landings secured the ports of Bandar Shahpur, Khorramshahr and the important refinery port of Abadan. On land, the 8th Indian Division crossed the Iraq border from Basra and reached Khorramshahr by 26 August. An advance into central Iran was halted by a strong Iranian defence at Ahvaz. Meanwhile, the 10th Indian Division invaded central Iran and faced stiff resistance in the mountainous terrain. After gaining air superiority, they broke through the Pai Tak Pass, opening the road to the capital Tehran.

The Soviets attacked north-western Iran in three columns (47th, 53rd and 44th armies) using 1000 tanks and substantial air support. The Caspian Sea Flotilla was also used to attack the Iranian Gilan Province. There was some resistance, particularly in Gilan but without armour or adequate air cover, the defences collapsed. The Soviets pressed on and in a few days, were threatening Tehran. By 29 August, the Iranian military situation was challenging, not helped by some incompetent generals and others who were pro-British. With several cities under Allied control and others threatened with bombing, Reza Shah sought an armistice. He was exiled to South Africa and replaced by Reza Pahlavi. The country was split between British and Soviet occupation forces for the rest of the war. The Anglo-Soviet-Persian Treaty of January 1942 provided for Iranian cooperation on internal security and other security measures, to stop German agents being infiltrated into the country from Turkey.[10] In 1943, US troops and personnel helped sustain the Persian corridor, which moved more than a quarter of Lend-Lease supplies to the Soviet Union.

Turkey strongly opposed the invasion diplomatically, regarding claims of German control as a pretext to gain military control of Iran. Some Turkish officials saw it as a precedent for Allied policy towards neutrals who failed to fall into line, even though the Allies were in no military position to take similar action against Turkey. Diplomatic notes from Britain and the Soviet Union promising to respect Turkish territorial integrity was an attempt to pacify the Turks and head off any possibility of Turkish intervention. The main Turkish concern was inviting the Soviet Union to participate, a point German propaganda used to claim Turkey would be the next Soviet target. The British Ambassador reported that this propaganda attack was effective.[11] The Turks were genuinely puzzled at Churchill's support for the Soviet Union, given his lifelong opposition to communism. Equally, the British never really understood the depth of Turkish concerns over the threat to them from the Soviets. This was reinforced by Soviet attempts to stir up the Kurdish tribes in eastern Turkey and claims that the Soviet Navy was sinking Turkish ships in the Black Sea.

**SOE Actions in Turkey**

Throughout the Iraq, Syria and Iran operations, the British were concerned that, despite Turkish neutrality, Axis supplies would be moved through the country. A memo from Commander in Chief Middle East (7 September 1941) states 'certain operations have been carried out against Axis supplies proceeding through Turkey to Iraq Syria and Iran during recent operations'.[12]

The Special Operations Executive (SOE) offered to deliver further small-scale actions if required, including:

- Minor sabotage to railways in Thrace
- Derailing trains in the Taurus tunnels
- Railway shops at Sivas and Adana
- Coal mines in the Zonguldak area
- German war material at Sansun and Trebizond
- Bridges over the Euphrates and in the Amanus area

These would be carried out by SOE operatives based at Aleppo and coordinated with an RAF bombing plan. They also planned to store equipment for these operations at the British consulate in Alexandretta and embassy stables in Therapia. The Commander in Chief's view was that these operations would be relatively ineffective owing to limited numbers and could only be carried out with the ambassador's approval. Nonetheless, it demonstrates a willingness to take covert action against Turkey at this time.

The idea was resurrected in April 1942.[13] The Commander in Chief Middle East argued that 'our present weakness makes SOE contribution more important'. They preferred diplomatic pressure, propaganda or the dispatch of forces to stiffen Turkish resistance. However, they recognised that covert sabotage could play a role, albeit with the risk of offending the Turks and defeating the object of the exercise. Planning included the dumping of explosives and sending 50 employees with construction parties. In conclusion, they 'felt the disadvantages outweigh the advantages at present and that we cannot, repeat cannot, run risk of alienating Turks at this time'.

SOE units inside Turkey also supported operations in Greece, which included a station at the port of Izmir. For example, they used Gerasimos Alexatos – a tobacco smuggler – as a courier using a caique out of Izmir, to liaise agents with in Greece.[14] This eventually led to attempts to block the Corinth Canal, which was used by the Italians to supply their garrisons in the Aegean. Other operations included blowing up the Italian transport ship *Hermada* in Piraeus harbour. Agents often fled to Turkey after such operations, which was also the source of supplies and forged documents.

SOE was not the only foreign intelligence force undertaking active operations in Turkey. On 24 February 1942, a bomb exploded behind Papen and his wife as they walked to work in Ankara, although neither was seriously injured. The assassin was a Turkish citizen born in Yugoslavia and he was killed in the explosion. The Turks claimed the Soviets trained him and even surrounded the Soviet embassy with an infantry battalion. They subsequently jailed two Soviet citizens and two Turkish accomplices. The Soviets claimed it was a German bomb as a pretext to invade Turkey and an 'out of favour' Papen was expendable. Neither explanations were particularly credible given the strategic position at the time. The Turks kept the investigation and court case secret, adding to the range of conspiracy theories.

**Pan-Turanism**

The German invasion of the Soviet Union opened up new opportunities for Turkey amongst the Turkic peoples of the Soviet Union. The Turkish ambassador to Berlin suggested that the Germans should organise these peoples into a Turanian state. He was invited to a discussion with the German High Command on the day of the Anglo-British invasion of Iran, which made him somewhat more circumspect.

İnönü himself was not opposed to pan-Turanism and often met with the Turkish Historical Society, a strong advocate of this policy. İnönü once joked that some members would not be satisfied until the Turkish frontier was pushed back to the walls of Vienna.[15] He also promoted known advocates of the cause. The Chief of Staff, Fevzi Çakmak, linked his anti-Soviet and pro-German sympathies to the cause. He is supposed to have gone as far as proposing buffer Turkic states carved out of Soviet territory.[16]

Saracoğlu in discussion with the Italian Ambassador to Ankara, indicated that if the British occupied part of Turkey, his country would make a common cause with Muslim Arabs. The British who were reading the decrypts of these reports would have viewed this as support for pan-Turanism and the Foreign Office Chief, Cadogan, was particularly concerned about the depth of support in the Turkish government.[17]

British sources also point to unofficial overtures on Turkish territorial revisionism in the Caucasus and Azerbaijan.[18] The British felt that more traditional territorial claims in Bulgaria, Iraq and the Dodecanese were more likely to surface at the war's end. The Turkish leadership used Nuri Pasha, the brother of Germany's old ally, Enver Pasha, who was visiting Germany to make the case. He defined pan-Turanian lands as the Crimea, Transcaucasia, Azerbaijan, the land between the Urals and the Volga River and Dagestan. He also claimed enclaves in Syria, Iraq and Iran. The Turanian state even stretched to the Chinese province of Sinkiang. The German Foreign Ministry, who hosted these discussions, was sympathetic and set up a special agency, although they questioned why Germany would want to cede control of the oilfields in these regions.

Turkey also made several approaches to the Germans, offering to insert themselves into the Balkans. One option was to send a neutral police force into Croatia and Albania to counter to Mussolini's plan to annex parts of Croatia and elsewhere into the Italian crown lands. The Germans were more concerned about the growing strength of partisan cells and believed stronger repression would be necessary. Unsurprisingly, the Italians mocked these initiatives.

The problem with pan-Turanism was that it required sustained German occupation of these regions, which was not achieved. In addition, while many Turks living under Soviet rule might want to escape Stalinism, they were not convinced Turkey would be much better. There was also the Armenians who would never agree to join a state headed by Turkey. Germany dropped the project in September 1942. Modern Turkish historians believe that while pan-Turanism had supporters in government,[19] it was more of a contingency plan, consistent with Turkish policy of keeping all options open. Notably, there were no Turkish equivalents of the Spanish units fighting on the Eastern Front or equivalent Waffen SS divisions.

**Allied Strategy – Arcadia**

On 7 December 1941, Japanese carrier-based aircraft attacked the US Pacific Fleet at Pearl Harbour; as President Roosevelt famously declared, 'a date which will live in infamy'. Later that day, the Japanese declared war on the USA and the British Empire and although they were under no obligation to do so under the Tripartite Pact, Germany and Italy also declared war on the USA.

The new Allies first met as coalition partners in Washington on 22 December 1941 at a conference codenamed Arcadia. This meeting agreed to a memorandum of understanding which set out the key principles of Allied strategy, including giving the defeat of Germany priority over other theatres of war. This was to be achieved by 'tightening the ring around Germany', which would be strengthened, by amongst other strategies, 'arming and supporting Turkey'. Except for the Russian Front, it was recognised that large scale land operations would not be practicable in 1942. However, there was a hope that in 1943, a return to the continent would be possible either through Scandinavia, northwest Europe or 'from Turkey into the Balkans'. This understanding would form the basis of differences over the Allied Mediterranean strategy and is crucial to understanding efforts to persuade Turkey to enter the war.

Only weeks after Arcadia, the then director of the War Plans Division of the US Army, Brigadier General Dwight Eisenhower, prepared a plan for the US Army's Chief of Staff, George Marshall, which outlined a series of potential operations in northwest Europe. The British were not impressed and Churchill was particularly scathing on the grounds that the Allies were not ready for such an undertaking. As no agreement could be reached on an invasion of France in 1942 and at least from a British perspective, in 1943, Operation Torch, the invasion of French North Africa, was agreed for the end of 1942. This committed the Allies to put large numbers of troops in the Mediterranean, which fitted in well with Churchill's strategic outlook. Once there, it would be difficult to move them for an invasion of France. Allied strategy, for now at least, was going to focus on forcing Italy out of the war and bringing Turkey into the conflict.

**Operation Gertrud**

This was the name given to a German plan to invade Turkey, prepared in the summer of 1942. It was planned to start from

Valentine Mark III tank. This tank was supplied in large numbers to the Soviet Union under Lend-Lease, who used them mainly on the Southern Front. They were later supplied to the Turkish Army. (Public Domain)

Greece and Bulgaria in the west, from Syria in the south and from the Caucasus. Hitler planned on establishing an Armenian state rather than supporting Turkey's concept of pan-Turanism. This new puppet state would control the oilfields of Azerbaijan, including Baku. Hitler said to Field Marshall Erich von Manstein that without the oilfields of Baku, the war is lost.[20]

Before the invasion of the Soviet Union, Germany was receiving about 51,000 tons of oil a month from the Soviets and most of this came from the Caucasus. These were the supplies that fuelled Blitzkrieg and ironically, Barbarossa as well. In July 1942, Hitler prioritised the conquest of the region above other strategic objectives favoured by OKH (Directive 41), including Moscow. Oil was his centre of gravity and he believed that whoever controlled the most oil resources would prevail. The Allied capture of Iran confirmed this view and holding the Caucasus would also cut off Lend-Lease supplies to the Soviets. The USA supplied 1,072 cargo trucks in August 1942 and 721 light bombers through this route by the end of 1942.[21] The Caucasus might also provide a base for expansion into Iran and Iraq. Albert Speer claimed that Hitler told him in August 1942, that his thrust to the Caucasus would lead to Iran and Iraq and then towards Afghanistan and India. This oil-driven strategic vision was aimed at ensuring Britain runs out of oil.[22]

The cutting edge of the German advance was one *Panzerarmee* commanded by von Kleist, which included three panzer divisions (3rd, 23rd and 13th) supported by the SS-Division Wiking, 1st Slovak Division and two Jager divisions. This would be followed 17 *Armee* commanded by Richard Ruoff with a mountain corps, two infantry corps and the Romanian 3rd Army. *Luftlotte* 4 (260 aircraft) would provide air cover and the *Kriegsmarine* would provide some limited naval support. The Soviet North Caucasus Front, led by Marshall Budyonny, would defend the region with five armies. However, many of these were understrength following earlier fighting in the Crimea and 42 percent of armoured support came from Lend-Lease tanks rather than T34's. Two Guards Rifle Divisions and four airborne brigades, provided veteran troops to shore up the defences. Just over 200 aircraft were available to support the Soviet forces, although many were obsolete types until the Lend-Lease planes arrived.

Von Kleist faced major logistical problems with only one rail line to supply his army and he was given two objectives: the mountain passes and the oilfields, which required different troop types. He had antiquated maps and no real understanding of the terrain, weather, or the vast distances his men would need to cover. Narrow but fast-flowing rivers provided key obstacles and the light wooden road bridges would struggle to handle heavy military traffic.

Despite early breakthroughs, these factors gradually ground down the advance which arrived in the Caucasus Mountains as the snow started to fall, blocking the high passes. The main effort was also diverted into costly urban fighting to capture the ports of Novorossiysk and Tuapse. Fuel supplies began to run out as the panzers reached the Grozny oilfields and fiercely contested river crossings further delayed von Kleist's army. Hitler increasingly intervened in tactical decisions after relieving the Army Group commander, von List, from his command.

As news of the Stalingrad victory boosted Soviet morale and diverted German reinforcements, Soviet counterattacks threatened to encircle the leading elements of the advance and von Kleist was authorised to make limited withdrawals. By January 1943, German forces were in full retreat back to the Kuban bridgehead and Rostov. Only a handful of oil rigs were made operational during the campaign extracting a mere 1,000 tons of oil at the cost of some 72,000 Axis casualties.

At the height of the campaign, Hitler wanted to bring U-Boats into the Black Sea to support his land campaign. Anticipating that the Turks would refuse a blatant breach of the Montreux Convention, he considered a scheme to dismantle the submarines at Linz in Austria and ship them down the Danube, reassembling them at the Romanian port of Constanta. This proved logistically too complex and a deal was suggested whereby for every U-Boat allowed through the Straits, one would be sold to Turkey. This did not happen but the Germans did provide other military equipment in return for raw materials at a later date.

Operation Gertrud was initially planned to start at the end of 1942. The failure of the Caucasus campaign and Stalingrad ended all thoughts of diverting troops to Thrace. Rommel's defeat at El Alamein

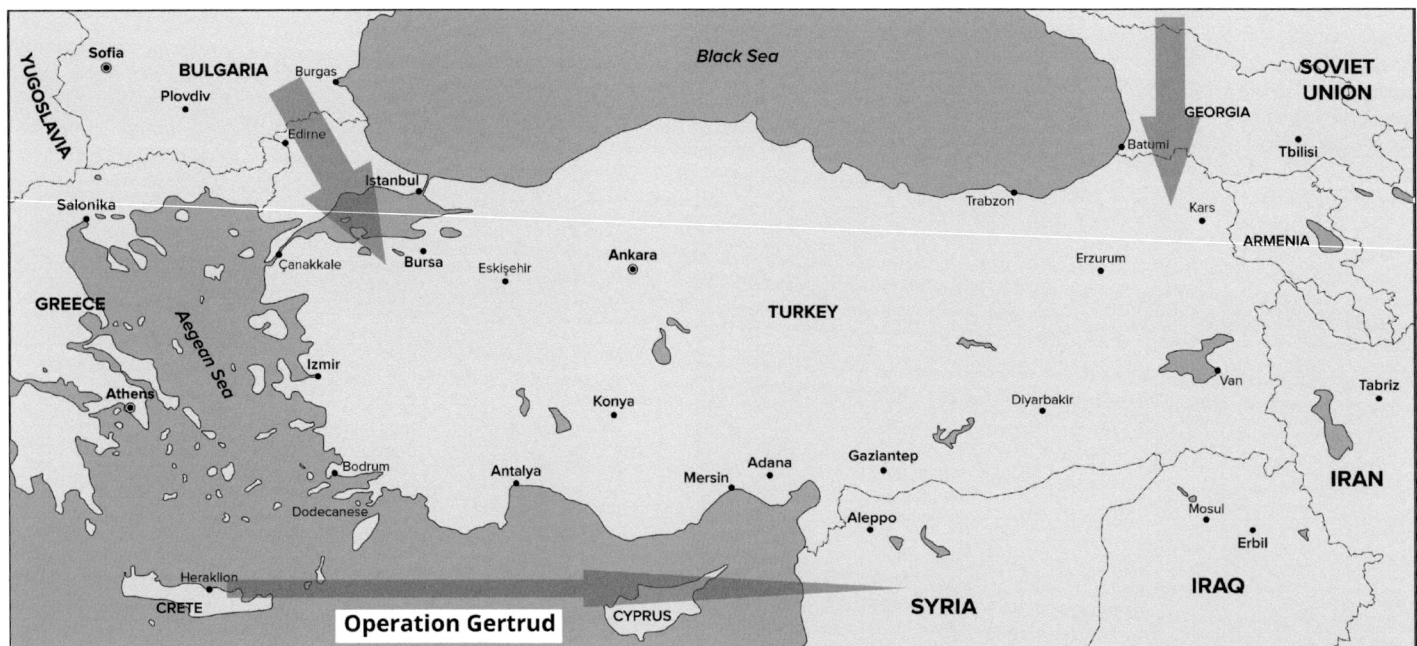

Operation Gertrud. (Author)

removed the southern push through Syria and Iraq. Although Turkey may not have realised it, any prospects of a German invasion had effectively gone by the end of 1942. In Berlin, the Japanese embassy identified another German concern with the plan, namely that it would bring the Royal Navy into the Black Sea, disrupting German operations in the Soviet Union.[23] In retrospect, Operation Gertrud looks pretty ambitious. However, these were the heady days of Blitzkrieg and other ambitious plans had been successful. Operation Gertrud had a big sister in the form of Operation Orient, which envisioned a link up with Japan through the Middle East. After the capture of the Caucasus and North Africa, they would link up with the Japanese in India. The plan was cancelled in early 1943.

The British did not think the plan was overly fanciful either. British military and political leaders all highlighted what they called the 'Northern Front' in the region, something often ignored in British history of the war, which focuses almost exclusively on North Africa. The Turks rightly believed that British plans would focus on a defence line along the Taurus Mountains, a natural defence line, rather than move troops into Anatolia to support Turkey. Japanese advances towards India strengthened these concerns of an Axis link up and the Turks believed this would also constrain Allied resources for Turkey. There is a British propaganda booklet published in July 1942,[24] 'Hitler's Last Hope', written in somewhat excitable language by Ernest Phillips and Noel Barber. The authors claimed, 'A mighty pincer movement to effect a link up with Japan across Asia, is Hitler's final desperate gamble. It has already begun. But in the Middle East, Turkey bars his way'. In essence, the authors make a case for aiding Turkey to resist this pincer movement.

In January 1943, the British launched a deception plan to keep German armoured units in the Balkans rather than North Africa. Operation Withstand spun a story that the Allies were so concerned about a German invasion of Turkey from Bulgaria, that they would divert the Axis by attacking Crete and the Dodecanese. A secondary aim was to emphasise to the Turks, the level of Allied concern to get them into the war. Amphibious forces were deployed in Cyprus and armoured units, including dummy tanks, went on manoeuvres along the Syrian border. German intelligence reported the inflated order of battle and identified 4.5 divisions were ready for operations in the Aegean and a further four and a half divisions poised for an invasion of Turkey.

*Hitler's Last Hope*, British propaganda booklet. (Author's Collection)

Allied concerns for the Northern Front was brought together in 1942 under 'Plan Wonderful'.[25] This recognised the limited Allied resources given the pressure Rommel was exerting in North Africa and the demands to transfer units to the Far East in response to the

Soviet-made tanks in Turkish service were T-26 Model 1932 (or T-26As, left), which had two turrets with DT machine guns calibre 7.62mm. Only four were delivered in 1932, to serve in the Tank Company (Training). Two years later, the Armoured Brigade was equipped with 64 T-26 Model 1933 (or T-26Bs), which had a single turret mounting one high-velocity 45mm gun and two DTs but no radio. The brigade was deployed in Thrace at the outbreak of the Second World War but saw no action: its T-26s remained in service until 1943. Sadly, the exact meaning of the insignia applied on the side remains unknown. (Artworks by David Bocquelet)

The Vickers Mk VIB was a British-made light tank first produced in 1936. It had a crew of three and was armed with a single .50-inch and one .303-inch Vickers machine gun. Turkey acquired 15 or 16 in 1940 and they served with the Armoured Brigade in Thrace. (Artwork by David Bocquelet)

The Renault R.35 was a French infantry support light tank. It was armed with one 37mm L/21 infantry gun and a 7.5mm machine gun. First produced in 1936, about 100 were acquired by Turkey in 1940. They equipped the Armoured Brigade's 1st and 2nd Tank Battalions in Thrace. (Artwork by David Bocquelet)

The M3A1 was a US-made light tank, produced starting in 1941. Turkey received 222 when the Allied Lend-Lease programme was expanded to the country, in 1943. They equipped four light tank battalions of the 1st and 2nd Armoured Brigades, deployed in Thrace and Gallipoli. Notably, this example received the insignia usually applied on aircraft of the Turkish air force but rarely on Army's vehicles. (Artwork by David Bocquelet)

The 'T.3' was the Turkish designation for the German designed and manufactured Panzerkampfwagen IIIJ (colloquially 'Panzer III'). This version had the short KwK 38 cannon calibre 50mm and two MG.34 machine guns calibre 7.92mm. Turkey acquired 34 in 1943, which equipped a tank battalion of the 6th Tank regiment, held in reserve in Ankara. As far as is known, all were painted in dark green overall. (Artwork by David Bocquelet)

The 'T.4' was the Turkish designation for the German designed and manufactured Panzerkampfwagen IVH. This version was equipped with the KwK 40 cannon calibre 75mm and two MG.34 machine guns calibre 7.92mm. Turkey acquired 37 in 1943 and they equipped a battalion of the 6th Tank Regiment held in reserve in Ankara. Like Panzer IIIs, they were all painted in dark green overall. (Artwork by David Bocquelet)

The Valentine Mk III was a British infantry tank manufactured since 1940. This version had a crew of four and was armed with a single 2-pdr (40mm) cannon and one BESA machine gun calibre 7.7mm. It was heavily armoured, with up to 65mm plates on the front. Turkey acquired almost 200, mainly from British army's stocks in the Middle East, in 1943. They equipped eight battalions of the 1st and 2nd Armoured Brigades based in Thrace and Gallipoli. (Artwork by David Bocquelet)

The Valentine MK IX was an up-gunned version of the Mk III: it still had a crew of four but was armed with a 6-pdr (57mm) gun and a BESA machine gun. Maximum armour thickness remained the same as on earlier variant. Turkey was supplied with around 30 in 1944 and they equipped the 2nd Battalion of the 1st Tank Regiment, based in Istanbul. (Artwork by David Bocquelet)

The second US-made tank to enter service with the Turkish Army was the M4A2 Sherman, the most-widely used Allied tank in the Second World War. This version had a 75mm cannon, a .50-inch and two .30-inch machine guns. Turkey was supplied with 27 Sherman tanks in 1944. They equipped the 1st Battalion of the 1st Tank Regiment, based in Istanbul. (Artwork by David Bocquelet)

The Polish-made PZL P-24 fighter was a gull-wing, all-metal fighter. It was armed with four machine guns and could carry four 12.5kg bombs. The P-24C series for Turkey consisted of 26 aircraft made by the PZL in Poland and 20 built under licence by the Kayseri aircraft factory in Turkey in 1936–1937. In 1940, they operated from Corlu AB, in Thrace, before moving to Kütahya, in western central Turkey. All were left in bare metal overall, had roundels in four position and their ruder painted in national colours. (Artwork by Peter Penev)

The Heinkel He.111 was a German bomber first produced in 1935. It could carry up to 2,000kg of bombs and was operated by the Condor Legion in the Spanish Civil War. A total of 24 He.111F-1s were exported to Turkey in 1938 and operated from Eskisehir AB, in north-western Turkey. Later on, the British helped with provision of spare parts from He.111s that crashed during the Battle of Britain. (Artwork by Peter Penev)

The British Bristol Blenheim was a light bomber first produced in 1937. It could carry up to 450kg of bombs but was used as a long-range fighter and night fighter by the RAF. London provided 30 Blenheims Mk 1 concurrently with the Turkish acquisition of He.111s. They were operated from Izmir Air Base, on the Aegean coast, starting in 1940. (Artwork by Goran Sudar)

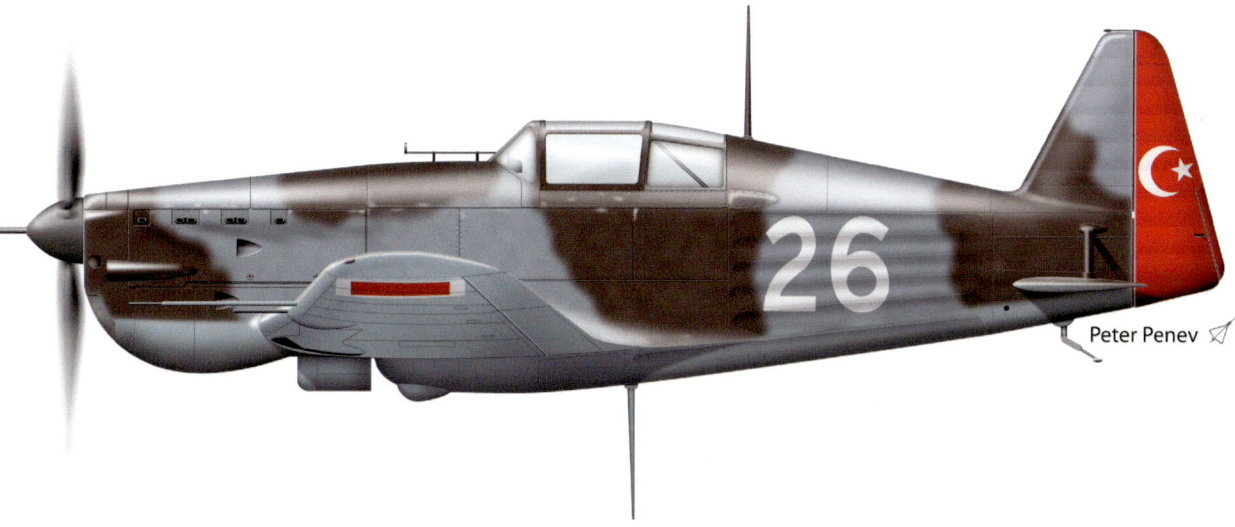

The Morane-Saulnier MS.406 was a modern, French-made fighter, introduced to service in 1938. It had a top speed of 489km/h at medium altitudes and was armed with a 20mm cannon and two machine guns. Turkey acquired a total of 45 MS.406C.1s and operated them from Izmir and Kütahya Air Bases. (Artwork by Peter Penev)

Westland Lysander was a British-made army cooperation aircraft, made famous later during the Second World War for its ability to land at night on very short, improvised airstrips behind enemy lines – usually to place, or to recover agents. Turkey bought 36 for close cooperation with ground forces, training and reconnaissance. (Artwork by Peter Penev)

The Curtis P-40 Tomahawk IIB was a US-made fighter operated by the RAF in the Middle East. It was armed with six 7.62mm machine guns and could carry a bomb of up to 100kg or a drop tank. The British supplied 36 Tomahawks under the Lend-Lease programme in 1941, from their stocks in the Middle East. Another 24 much improved P-40D Kittyhawks were provided in 1942. They were primarily operated from Izmir Air Base. (Artwork by Peter Penev)

The Martin Baltimore was a US-made light bomber introduced in 1941. It could carry up to 910kg of bombs and some variants were armed with a total of 11 to 13 machine guns calibre 7.62mm. A total of 72 Baltimore Mk I and II versions were supplied to Turkey in 1944, to re-equip bomber units. They were primarily operated from Eskisehir and Kütahya Air Bases. (Artwork by Peter Penev)

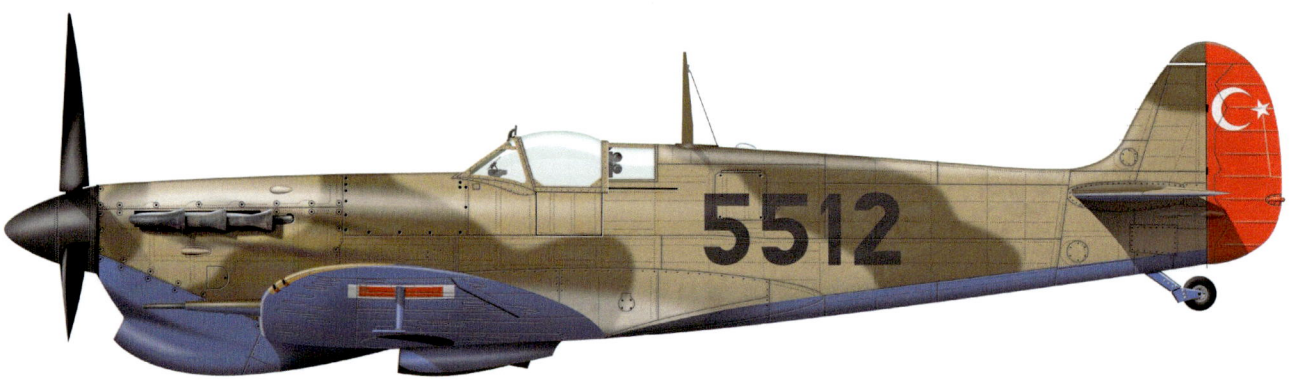

The Supermarine Spitfire was the leading British fighter of the Second World War and one manufactured in greatest numbers. Turkey ordered 14 before the Second World War but only one was delivered: in 1944, the British then provided 104 Spitfire Mk Vs, each armed with two 20mm cannons and four machine guns. They were mainly based at Merzifon Air Base, in northern Turkey and in Izmir. (Artwork by Goran Sudar)

In September 1942, Germany agreed to provide one of its best fighters, the Focke Wulf Fw.190A-3 to Turkey, in an effort to keep the country neutral. They began arriving the same year, all armed with four 20mm cannons and two machine guns. They were allocated to the defence of the Straits and based at Bursa Air Base. (Artwork by Goran Sudar)

# CHASING THE SOFT UNDERBELLY: TURKEY AND THE SECOND WORLD WAR

This illustration shows a typical infantryman in a rifle platoon of the Turkish Army in the summer uniform, frequently described as, 'very shoddy, ill-fitting clothes' and made in a khaki-coloured canvass material. The most common rifle was the First World War vintage Mauser M.88 or 98. (Artwork by Renato Dalmaso)

This was a Turkish infantry officer, usually described as 'invariably smartly dressed and well turned out'. Turkish officer uniforms were made by private tailors of a dark olive drab material. Badges of rank were shown on shoulder straps. (Artwork by Renato Dalmaso)

Each infantry battalion of the Turkish Army had a machine gun company of three platoons. They typically consisted of three Maxim 08 Schwarzlose 7.92mm HMGs. This crew is shown wearing the winter uniform and overcoat described as, 'a rough, shoddy, grey mixture, woollen serge uniform'. (Artwork by Renato Dalmaso)

Map drawn by Tom Cooper.

Japanese advances. This plan envisaged 26 RAF squadrons and four brigade groups from the British Ninth Army moving into southern Anatolia, whilst a more substantial force, including armoured divisions, would prepare defensive positions in the Taurus region. The key points would be the railway lines that the Germans would need to move from Turkey into the Middle East. In practice, there was little prospect of the units allocated to even this limited plan, being available. Abandoning most of Turkey to the Axis would have confirmed the Turks worst fears about Allied commitments to their defence.

### No Stars to Guide

Finally, a story that captures Turkey during this period rather well. 'No Stars to Guide' is the title of Adrian Seligman's account of his Second World War exploits as a Royal Navy Reserve officer taking a Russian oil tanker from Istanbul to Beirut in early 1942. Whilst Turkey was neutral and he would largely stay within Turkish territorial waters, the journey back to a British base involved sailing past the German and Italian occupied Aegean and Dodecanese islands.

There was some informal cooperation from the Turkish authorities but German intelligence was active in attempting to stop the ships leaving. Eventually, they received clearance to leave and Seligman joined his ship, called the *Olinda*, which was crewed by an eclectic mix of White Russians, Arabs, Chinese and Maltese sailors. He had to communicate mostly in French. The previous ship movement had been torpedoed by the Germans just outside the Dardanelles. The plan for the *Olinda* was to disguise it as a Turkish cargo ship and sail down the coast in daylight.

The *Olinda* got through the Dardanelles barrage at the second go and made its way down the coast. The disguise did not last long. The ship was attacked by German aircraft and Seligman had to revert to the original plan of sailing at night and laying up during the day. This involved some challenging sailing along the rocky coast. The Axis forces frequently ignored Turkish neutrality by crossing into their waters but so did the British. When Seligman thought they were through the worse, the ship grounded on sandbanks, as the charts were always vague on these features. However, they eventually got free and avoided the Axis searching forces yet again to break into the open sea and safety.

His story is not only a good read but it also shows how Turkish neutrality on the coast was treated by both combatants and the Turks themselves.

# 7
# DIPLOMACY AND DECEPTION 1943–1944

Many histories of the Second World War describe the start of 1943 as 'turning the tide'. In North Africa, Rommel was trapped in Tunisia after the Battle of El Alamein and Operation Torch landings in Morocco and Algeria. On the eastern front, the Battle of Stalingrad halted the German offensive with the surrender of the German 6th Army on 2 February. However, from a neutral's perspective like Turkey, the war still looked to be in the balance, albeit tilting in the Allies favour.

The Germans, particularly Ribbentrop, despite Papen's best efforts, were becoming convinced that Turkey was not a genuine neutral. The Adana conference was a strong indication of this shift to Ribbentrop and spy reports of British troops on training and construction duties in Turkey. Papen was concerned that Ribbentrop was mounting a campaign to justify war against Turkey and he may not have been aware of the Operation Gertrud plan.

The British believed that Allied success had impressed the Turks and remained sceptical about Turkish concerns over a German invasion. They argued that Axis units in Greece and the Aegean were mostly Italian and any invasion would require a significant shift of German divisions from other fronts. With support from Brooke, Churchill moved to a much more optimistic view of getting Turkey into the war, which reflected his long-standing view on the importance of Turkey and the best strategy for winning the war. This was despite intercept evidence that indicated the Turks remained intent on staying neutral.

The British encouraged the Turks diplomatically with discussions on a Balkan bloc while emphasising that a Turkish role depended on Turkey entering the war, not simply participating afterwards. The governments in exile were less enthusiastic given their experience in 1940–1941 but this did not stop Turkey from promoting peace initiatives with the Axis satellite states in the Balkans. As usual, this was driven by Turkish concerns over the Soviet Union. The British found out about these initiatives through intercepts and discouraged them because of the damage they could do to the alliance with the Soviet Union.

### Mediterranean Strategy

The key factor for engaging Turkey in the war would be the Allied strategy for defeating the Axis. In simple terms, would the Allies pursue an indirect approach based on the Mediterranean, favoured by Churchill, or would they go straight for the jugular, with an invasion of North-West Europe, as favoured by the Americans? In the former, Turkey would be a key player; in the latter, Turkey would be almost irrelevant.

The Mediterranean strategy during the Second World War has been the subject of some controversy, both during and after the war. The eminent British historian, Sir Michael Howard, published a series of lectures he gave in 1966,[1] which provides a concise appreciation of the debate. He also had some practical experience of this theatre of war, having landed at Salerno as an infantry platoon commander in September 1943. He takes the reader through the various stages and analyses the differences between British support for striking the 'soft underbelly' of Europe against the American preference for decisive action in North-West Europe.

The controversy between the different strategies was stoked by the High-Tory historian Sir Arthur Bryant's volumes on the war,[2] which drew from Lord Alan Brooke's papers, claiming the Americans were to blame for not liberating Eastern Europe. Subsequent publications played down the differences and by 1963 the American scholar Richard Leighton concluded that the Balkans versus Western Europe controversy was a myth.[3] This might be somewhat overdoing it. As Howard shows, from 1940 to at least early 1944, Churchill and several British commanders did favour a more aggressive strategy in the Mediterranean. The Washington conference in December

1941, which set the Allied strategy, included a reference to a tightening of the ring around Germany, including the possibility of using Turkey to access the Balkans.

In 1943, British planners were reluctant to withdraw divisions from the Mediterranean for use in North-West Europe and made a case for exploiting an invasion of Italy into the Balkans through a Dalmatian bridgehead. There were active discussions with Turkey, although their prevarication indicated that this might not be fruitful. Churchill, as late as July and October 1943, was making a case for the Mediterranean to take precedence over Overlord. In May 1944, he told the Dominion Prime Ministers he favoured rolling up Europe from the Balkans but he had been unable to persuade the Americans. The US Chief of Staff, George Marshall, was the strongest opponent of Churchill on this issue. At a US post-Torch strategy meeting on 10 December 1942, Roosevelt indicated that he wanted to keep the options open. In response, Marshall described operations in the Mediterranean as 'dabbling' and his view prevailed. At the later Sextant conference, Marshall went so far as to threaten to pull out of Europe and focus on the Pacific if the British ditched Overlord in favour of the Mediterranean.

The lower slopes of the mountains above Caporetto, which gives a flavour of the challenges facing an Allied advance. (Photo by Author)

The Germans provide some support for Churchill's view of the Mediterranean strategy, at least in the early stages. General Warlimont of the OKW described the Tunisian campaign as the most decisive of the war, opening up the weak Axis southern flank.[4] Operation Torch also resulted in the Germans occupying the whole of France, adding another 400 miles of coastline to be defended and another army of occupation. The German reaction to later operations in the Dodecanese and Italy involved deploying additional ground and air units because Hitler feared an assault through the Balkans. In a practical sense, real and deception operations did draw many more German divisions into the Mediterranean, as Hitler was more concerned about losing the Balkan mineral resources than Italy. By the end of 1943, there were 25 divisions in Italy and a further 20 in the Balkans. While Hitler publicly trumpeted the benefits of getting the Italians out of the way, Goebbels, in his diary, highlighted the impact the divisions sent to Italy could have had on the Eastern Front. He noted that the unconditional surrender of the Italians had come at minimal cost to the Allies.

Despite Alan Brooke's diary notes, Howard argues that the Americans had at no point insisted on abandoning the Mediterranean; they simply favoured the agreed plan of focusing on northwest Europe. The American position was that logistics and terrain precluded decisive operations into the heart of Europe from the Mediterranean. They did not want to jeopardise the overall strategy just to exploit local successes in what they viewed as a secondary theatre. Alan Brooke makes it clear in his diaries that he did not support Churchill's Balkan ambitions, even if the Americans thought he did.[5] Although later in November 1943, he notes that he wishes he had been more persuasive with the Americans over capturing Crete and Rhodes, which he thought could have led to the Allies forcing the Dardanelles and pushing on into the Balkans. Even General Alexander commanding British troops in Italy, pointed to the difficulties of attacking Germany from the south. Howard argues that the rivers and mountain passes, including the so-called Ljubljana Gap, were formidable obstacles, which would be defended by the Germans all the way. Planners with any grasp of history will have recalled the 12 battles around the Isonzo River, near Trieste, during the First World War. The first 11 resulted in 750,000 casualties amongst Austro-Hungarian and Italian troops. The final battle, Caporetto, almost resulted in the Italians crashing out of the war when 250,000 Italians were taken prisoner.

It is undeniable that there were differences in approach between the Allies on this issue. The Americans struggled to hold the British to the agreed strategy, while British caution about a precipitate attack over the Channel was well-founded. Howard concluded that a compelling case has still to be made for there being any faster or economical way of winning the war.

### Casablanca Conference

Whatever the differences in overall strategy, in early 1943, there were few options other than action in the Mediterranean. Substantial Allied forces had already been committed to the area, with no prospect of transferring the necessary shipping to launch an invasion over the Channel in 1943. The experience from the failed Dieppe raid in 1942 had reinforced the view that there may not be a 'soft underbelly' but it was a better option than northwest Europe for now. Most importantly, the focus was on supporting the Soviets. In 1943, the Mediterranean was the only theatre of war that could relieve the pressure on them and obviate the risk that Stalin might make a separate peace with Hitler.

In January 1943, Churchill and Roosevelt met to plan Allied grand strategy at Casablanca. Stalin declined to attend due to the ongoing Battle of Stalingrad, although his fear of flying and security concerns made his attendance unlikely. The conference is best known for the declaration of 'unconditional surrender', largely

Casablanca Conference, 14–24 January 1943. President Franklin D. Roosevelt, Prime Minister Winston S. Churchill and their combined Chiefs of Staff at the Casablanca Conference. Standing, (left to right): General Brehon B. Somervell; General H.H. Arnold; Admiral Ernest J. King; unidentified; General George C. Marshall, Admiral Sir Dudley Pound; General Sir Alan Brooke; Sir Charles Portal; and Vice Admiral Louis Mountbatten. (National Museum of the US Navy)

driven (again) by Roosevelt's concerns that Stalin might make peace. However, the more immediate concern was the next steps in the war. George Marshall, the US Army Chief of Staff wanted a cross channel invasion in 1943, although his planners were pessimistic and the US Navy and air force chiefs were open to persuasion otherwise. His British counterpart, Sir Alan Brooke, argued for an invasion of Sicily to force Italy out of the war, which would compel Germany to occupy the Italian peninsula and replace the Italian forces in the Balkans and the Dodecanese as well. The compromise was a firm commitment to an invasion of France in 1944, coupled with British troops and resources going to Burma to support the war in the Far East. This satisfied the US Navy chief, Admiral King, responsible for the Pacific War because he had the resources allocated for his 1943 objectives. Not that all American military leaders thought it was much of a compromise. As General A C Wedemeyer put it, 'We came, we listened and we were conquered'.

The air plans agreed at Casablanca included the strategic bombing of the Romanian airfields at Ploesti, although it was a low priority. However, if the necessary bases could be secured, especially in Turkey, the bombing of Romania would present comparatively little difficulty. The British were also making a case for an operation against the Dodecanese to encourage Turkey's entry into the war. For this reason, they were keener on attacking Sardinia (Operation Brimstone) than Sicily (Operation Husky) because the former would release spare resources for this operation. However, shipping and air objections led to Sicily being selected.

The Casablanca conference agreed that getting Turkey into the war should be solely in the hands of the British. Churchill asked that the British be allowed to play the Turkish hand, just as the United States was handling China. The British would keep the United States informed at all times. The plan was to transform the defensive agreement with Turkey into an offensive one. This led to discussions about what operations would need to be mounted to reassure the Turks against the fear of an Axis counterattack. 10th Army based in the Nile Delta would be available even during Operation Husky and there was no longer the risk of a German incursion from the Caucasus. Operations, as Churchill put it, 'to encourage and support the Turks'. Initial British plans included an attack on Rhodes and the Dodecanese. Crete was regarded as too difficult. For these operations, they argued that airfield facilities in Turkey would be a considerable help. However, as all shipping and air support was committed to Husky, it would only be possible to exploit these opportunities if Turkey entered the war.[6]

The planners did consider territorial inducements for Turkey, although the Joint Planning Staff advised against obtaining allies by bribery given experience during the First World War. It was argued that Turkey was remaining neutral, not out of greed but out of fear of the dwindling threat of Axis invasion and the growing menace of Russian ambitions. The Joint Planners suggested that, 'we should make it clear to Turkey that our good offices at the Peace Conference will depend on her entry into the war without delay' and that adequate military equipment should be offered to bring her defensive forces up to strength. They also regarded Turkey as primarily a base for air operations and to use the Dardanelles to help supply Russia. This was enough for Churchill to determine that no effort should be spared to bring Turkey into the war and to plan his own future movements accordingly.

### Adana Conference

The Mediterranean strategy involved more aggressive efforts to encourage Turkey to join the war and Churchill was prepared to meet the Turkish leadership to achieve this personally. The British War Cabinet was not enthusiastic, with Attlee and Eden arguing that the meeting was likely to fail.[7]

The Adana conference was held in a railway carriage at Yenice railway station. The event is marked today with a billboard on the station building. (Photo by Nedim Ardoğa)

General Henry Maitland (Jumbo) Wilson was the British General Officer Commanding Middle East Command and the main Allied link with the Turkish military. (via William Cobb)

The conference took place in a railway carriage at Yenice railway station near the Turkish city of Adana on 30–31 January 1943. In addition to İsmet İnönü and Winston Churchill, Turkey was represented by Prime Minister Şükrü Saracoğlu, Foreign Minister Numan Menemencioğlu, Field Marshal Fevzi Çakmak and a group of advisers. The British team had Harold Alexander, Henry Maitland Wilson, Sir Alan Brooke, Sir Wilfred Lindsell, Alexander Cadogan (Foreign Office), Air Marshal Drummond and Commodore Dundas. Harold Alexander was about to take over 18 Army Group in Tunisia, a step up from his last trip to Turkey in command of an Irish Guards battalion in Constantinople in 1922. His battalion occupied the Chataldja lines to deter a Greek plan to occupy the city, – so he had some understanding of the Turkish position.[8]

Churchill recognised the concerns of his Cabinet colleagues and had quite limited aims for the conference. In an explanatory message to Commonwealth Prime Ministers, he explained that the objective was to strengthen Turkey to get them into the war at a later stage.[9] Churchill was also well aware of Turkish concerns about the Soviet Union. Saracoğlu had told him that all of Europe would be communist if Germany were beaten,[10] and İnönü even suggested bringing the war to an end before Germany's unconditional surrender to avoid a Soviet move towards the Mediterranean. Churchill suggested that Turkey could best secure its future as a victorious belligerent, which left the implied threat to their security if they did not take that step. In a later discussion with General Wilson, Churchill was more explicit, saying that if Turkey refused these facilities, there would follow 'every form of pressure which it is in our power to exert, including letting the army supply peter out and withdrawing all guarantees by Britain and Russia for the maintenance of the status quo'.

Even without a declaration of war, Churchill wanted facilities in Turkey to attack the Ploesti oilfields, the Dodecanese and access through the Dardanelles to the Black Sea. The Turkish leadership expressed sympathy for the Allied cause but little else, arguing that facilities in the Straits would be a breach of the Montreux Convention. Sir Alan Brooke left the meeting with some optimism, although he later recognised his optimism was not justified and doubted if Turkish forces could ever have been trained up to the necessary standards. Churchill and the Foreign Office were more sceptical and this is reflected in Churchill's statement in the House of Commons when he said:

Whereas a little while ago it looked to superficial observers as if Turkey might be isolated by a German advance through the Caucasus on one side and by a German-Italian attack on Egypt on the other, a transformation has occurred. Turkey now finds on each side of her, victorious Powers who are her friends. It will be interesting to see how the story unfolds chapter by chapter and it would be very foolish to try to skip on too fast.

The British Naval Attaché in Ankara, after meeting the Deputy Chief of the Turkish General Staff, reported that the 'General Staff appear more isolationist than ever'. He thought they hoped the Germans and Soviets would wear each other out. The Italian ambassador to Turkey took a similar view.[11] It was agreed that military experts would meet to discuss Turkey's equipment requirements. The British aim was to enable the Turkish Army to resist and attack and so feel able to grant the Allies the facilities they required. General Wilson visited Ankara on 18 April 1943 and was told firmly by

The German Panzer IV tank was supplied to Balkan allies as well as Turkey where it was classified as the T4. (Photo by Author, Belgrade Kalemegdan)

Marshal Çakmak that Turkey would enter the war only if she felt imminently threatened by either Russia or Germany. The Turks wanted to focus on the amount of equipment, while the British were interested in its purpose and use. As Edward Weisband puts it 'Operation Footdrag' had begun.[12]

The trip to Adana was an extraordinary security risk for Churchill, which again demonstrates his commitment to the Turkish project. Alan Brooke was singularly unimpressed with the Turkish sentries, who he found hunkered down with a blanket over their heads. There is some evidence from decrypts of an attempt by the Germans to assassinate him on the return journey.[13] This plot involved an attack at Algiers or Casablanca by Islamic militants. The Deputy PM, Clement Attlee, advised Churchill of the threat and recommended a different route home.

The US built M3 Stuart equipped the light tank companies of the Turkish 1st and 2nd Armoured Brigades. (Photo by Mark Holloway)

### Operation Hardihood and the Turkish Armed Forces

One of the achievements of Turkish policy was the ability to secure military equipment from both sides. In September 1942, Turkey was granted a loan of 100 million Reichsmarks for arms, a move that surprised the British and is quite extraordinary given the German position at the time. However, it was linked to the essential export of chromite from Turkey to Germany. Among other military supplies, this bought 34 Pkw IIIJ and 37 Pkw IVH tanks. These were known as T3 and T4 in Turkish service and equipped the 6th Tank Regiment, held in reserve at Ankara. This also allowed the foreign minister, Menemencioğlu, to develop a policy he called 'active neutrality', which allowed Turkey to offer to mediate at the Adana conference. An offer that the Allies unsurprisingly rejected.

Operation Hardihood was the British code name for support to Turkey in the form of British formations, military equipment and broader economic assistance. The equipment provided was in response to a very long list of Turkish requirements, which they could not possibly have incorporated into their existing forces. These included 1,470 heavy and 855 other tanks, 2,600 guns and

The British Daimler Dingo Scout Car equipped the reconnaissance companies of the Turkish armoured brigades. (Photo by Joost J. Bakker)

One of the 6-pdr ATGs supplied to Turkey. (Photo by Author, Istanbul Military Museum)

Stuart light tanks, 25 Sherman medium tanks, 150 Dingo scout cars, 59 Bren carriers and 48 Bishop self-propelled guns. This allowed the Turkish army to reorganise their armoured forces into three armoured brigades, equipped with Allied armour, facing the Balkans.

- 1st Armoured Brigade (Istanbul) – 2nd & 3rd Tank Regiments
- 2nd Armoured Brigade (Gelibolu) – 4th & 5th Tank Regiments
- 3rd Armoured Brigade (Istanbul) – 1st Tank Regiment

An armoured brigade also had an attached artillery regiment with a battalion of 12 25-pdr field guns and a battalion of 12 Bishop SPGs. There was also a reconnaissance company with 23 Dingo scout cars. Tank regiments typically had two battalions, each with two companies of nine Valentine tanks and one of nine Stuart light tanks.

Infantry divisions also received almost 100,000 items of small arms, including Lee-Enfield rifles, Sten and Thompson sub-machine guns, 81mm mortars, PIAT anti-tank launchers. Artillery included 40mm Bofors AA guns, 3.7inch AA guns, 6-pdr ATGs, plus British and American trucks and jeeps. Turkish infantry could also be seen wearing British helmets, some of which were still in use as late as the Cyprus conflict in 1974.

howitzers, 1,198 aircraft and enough fuel for 30 times their annual consumption. The naval requests would have required the Turks to double the size of their navy. One American official in Ankara said, to supply the Turks with everything they wanted would be like 'feeding an eight course dinner to an eight-day-old baby'.

Churchill urged his planners to do their best to supply the Turks even if this caused some 'slight indigestion'. He argued that Turkey's port and transportation systems would limit what could be supplied. As the Axis effectively blockaded Smyrna from their bases in the Dodecanese, supplies had to be imported along Turkey's limited railway system from small ports like Iskanderun on the south coast. This excuse had the added advantage of encouraging the Turkish military to assist in a campaign to capture the Dodecanese.

The Allied Lend-Lease equipment supplied to Turkey as part of this programme would primarily come from surplus stocks in North Africa. They included 180 (50 more to follow) Valentine tanks, 222

The air force received modern aircraft including 60 Hurricane IIB and C, 19 Blenheim bombers and 15 Beaufighters. The British had previously supplied 36 P-40 Tomahawk fighters at the end of 1941 and 1942. The Germans had refused to provide spare parts for Heinkel bombers and the Turks received parts from crashed bombers in Britain. Similar problems were encountered with French and Polish aircraft, which added to the air force's already low efficiency. A small number of US Liberator bombers crash-landed in Turkey following raids on Ploesti in 1942 and 1943. Four of these were repaired and constituted a heavy bomber 'squadron' based at Eskisehir with others used for spare parts.[14]

The British supplied generic equipment including flying suits, cameras, parachutes and airfield construction materials. They also provided one million rounds of ammunition per month and some bombs. Even more importantly, Standard Oil provided aviation fuel after Romanian supplies were diverted to Germany. Britain built 38 airfields, including 15 all-weather fields near the Straits, using engineers and construction workers sent from the UK. Ironically, the US added these airfields to their target list in 1942 when the Allies thought Turkey might join the Axis. The nearest Axis airbases in 1943 were on Rhodes with four airfields and some 200 planes. However, the Turkish air force had no bases opposite Rhodes, with the nearest field being at Izmir.

The Turkish Navy received relatively little equipment. Two Demirhisar Class (modified Royal Navy I Class) destroyers were delivered in 1942. Two others intended for Turkey were taken over by the Royal Navy on completion and one was returned in 1945. Two Oruc Reis Class (Modified Royal Navy S Class) submarines were delivered in 1942 and again, the Royal Navy took over the other two planned deliveries. In a rare war loss, the submarine fleet had lost the TCG *Atilay*, built in Istanbul to a German design, on 14 July 1942. The submarine was lost testing underwater magnetic security lines in the Dardanelles. It was raised in 1994 and a 4.9-foot hole in the hull proved that she hit a naval mine. It is assumed that the mine was a First World War munition, laid during the Dardanelles Campaign.

In addition to equipment, the British provided extensive training for Turkish troops in Turkey and the Middle East. A June 1943 training progress report includes courses on tanks, artillery, anti-aircraft and engineering, in very significant numbers.[15] The RAF also provided flying and technical training for the Turkish air force. The effectiveness of this training was questioned in a damming report by Colonel Sleeman based on his visit to Turkey on 4–9 June 1943.[16] He said;

The US built Curtis P-40 fighters were supplied to Turkey from British Middle East stocks. (USAF)

Four I Class destroyers were ordered by the Turkish Navy but two were purchased by the Royal Navy. The Turkish I-class ships were of a similar design to their British counterparts but shipped only eight torpedoes. (Royal Navy Official Photographer, Public Domain)

General Salih Omurtak on board HMS *Formidable* during his April 1943 visit to Allied forces in the Western Mediterranean. He went on to become the Chief of the General Staff of the Turkish Armed Forces on 1 August 1946. (Public Domain)

This training will not be carried out without leadership and enthusiasm, both of which are totally lacking in the superior hierarchy of the Turkish army ... Turkish senior officers, who do not want or try to understand. They are conceited, they continue to live in the glories of the War of Independence, give blind obedience to the Marshal and demand it of the army. They fear modern training methods, have so far proved incapable of being trained and have not admitted the need for training.

The report assessed that only around 20 percent of the training effort had been usefully absorbed. Matters were slightly better in the armoured schools but he highlighted the age of officers, Majors averaged 50 and Colonels between 55 and 60, as a problem because they tended to cramp the initiative of the younger junior officers. After training, there was no follow-up because Turkish law did not allow foreign troops to be attached to operational units. This meant that units moved from their base areas with insufficient drivers and no engineering or spare parts. It was even worse in artillery units, with the troops focused on how smart the equipment looked rather than being able to fire them. Mechanics were incapable of doing basic repairs to vehicles.

In conclusion, Colonel Sleeman advised that no progress would be made until the Turkish army had been purged and reorganised on modern lines. British instructors' time was wasted and the weapons provided had been neglected and ill-treated. Allowing that this is the view of only one senior officer, it does indicate that simply providing modern equipment was unlikely to be enough to turn the Turkish army into an effective fighting force.

The Americans had also stepped up their engagement with the Turkish armed forces. US technicians had been in Turkey since the early 1940s and an expanded role was specifically aimed at countering German influence. American officers taught on aviation courses and at the War School and Navy School.[17] For Turkey, the USA had the benefit of gaining technical expertise without the imperial interests of the British or the Germans. Students and cadets also went to the USA, some of which had been recalled from Germany because of concerns about indoctrination into Nazi ideology. Military observers visited the Allied fronts in North Africa, including a mission under General Salih Omurtak to Tunisia. Turkish journalists were also included in the propaganda offensive with invitations to visit the USA. American films began to dislodge Germans in Turkish cities and in the military academies and a cultural attaché was sent to Ankara in 1944. The hard military equipment was largely coming from British stocks but the Americans were engaging in, what we would call these days, soft power.

Operation Hardihood also envisaged formed British units in Turkey if they entered the war. These included 25 RAF squadrons with anti-aircraft artillery to protect the airfields and three anti-tank regiments. Further waves would bring a further 25 RAF squadrons, three anti-tank regiments and even two armoured divisions. However, it is clear in reports from the British Ambassador and others that the Turks had no intention of joining the war.

## Operation Barclay and Sicily

One of the greatest, if less well known, British successes of the Second World War, was strategic deception. These operations did not just aim to conceal or mislead the Axis; they had to persuade them to act. Churchill was a big supporter of this approach. On 14 October 1939, the German U-47 had crept into Scapa Flow and sank the battleship HMS *Royal Oak*. As First Lord of the Admiralty, Churchill visited Scapa Flow and ordered the construction of dummy ships to deceive enemy reconnaissance aircraft. He even ordered sailors to drop refuse around them to attract seagulls, 'Feed the gulls and fool the Germans', he said.

British strategic deception enjoyed two huge advantages. The first was signals intelligence, primarily the decrypting of the German High Command cyphers through Ultra and, as Denniston's study shows, diplomatic decrypts.[18] The second was the security of the United Kingdom, including the control of all active agents in Britain.[19] While the second advantage was less obvious in the Eastern Mediterranean, by 1943, the Luftwaffe had limited aerial reconnaissance capacity to check on the information being fed to them by human and signals intelligence sources.

General Wavell established a deception unit in Cairo early in the war called 'A' Force, run by Colonel Dudley Clarke. Wavell had seen and written about the deception operations used by General Allenby in Palestine during 1917–1918. He grasped the important role that deception and surprise can play in military operations, particularly when you are outnumbered and far from home bases. Early operations in East Africa tested techniques including dummy administration, radio traffic, rumours and calculated intelligence leaks, which persuaded the Italians to concentrate their forces in

'Sunshield' split cover, one half on, one half off a tank in the workshops at Middle East Command Camouflage Development and Training Centre, Helwan, Egypt, 1941. (British Middle East Command Directorate of Camouflage, Public Domain)

the wrong place. Unlike their German counterparts, the officers engaged in deception operations were fully integrated into the operational staffs of commanders in the field.

In October 1941, Clarke had run a story (Agent Cheese) that the Operation Crusader offensive was postponed because three British divisions were being sent to the Caucasus to help the Russians, supported by three divisions from India. Clarke managed to get himself arrested in Madrid shortly afterwards dressed as a woman. The Director of Counter Espionage at MI5, understandably took a dim view of such risky behaviour and it remains unclear if this was professional or personal behaviour.[20] Either way, Lord Gort, the Governor of Gibraltar, was told to investigate and he decided to send Clarke back to the Middle East. This was a close shave for both Clarke and the future of British deception in the Mediterranean.

Officers of HMS *Seraph*, which floated the corpse off the coast of Spain during Operation Mincemeat. (Pelman, L (Lt), Royal Navy Official Photographer, Public Domain)

Neutral Turkey played a key role in deception operations using the military attaches in Ankara (Arnold) and Istanbul (Wolfson). Clarke visited Turkey in April 1941 to set up the systems that operated throughout the war. A key task was to create bogus units to give a misleading view of Allied strength. This started with Operation Cascade in March 1942, which created one armoured and seven phoney infantry divisions. By 1943, they had added eight more infantry and three armoured divisions to the fictional order of battle. Sustaining a credible threat in the eastern Mediterranean was a key part of Allied strategy for the rest of the war, even when the real action had shifted westwards.

Operation Barclay was a deception plan which aimed to convince the Axis that the Allies would invade the Balkans and Sardinia rather than the actual attack on Sicily (Operation Husky), building on the work undertaken in Operation Withstand earlier in 1943. This force would attack Crete then the Peloponnese, bringing Turkey into the war by attacking Bulgaria and Romania. It created a fictitious 12th Army in the Eastern Mediterranean consisting of 12 divisions complete with landing craft and air support. Turkish intelligence was not told this build-up of troops was a deception operation.

The deception plans included engineers fabricating dummy landing craft and 11 dummy fighter squadrons (Operation Waterfall), double agents feeding the Abwehr false information, fake troop movements, radio traffic and the recruitment of Greek troops.[21] Appeals were made for Greek interpreters and large amounts of Greek drachmas were bought in Cairo, together with printed maps and pamphlets about Greece. Extensive air plans were developed for the eastern Mediterranean to keep busy the estimated 310 Axis aircraft deployed there.[22] There was also a detailed schedule of dummy and actual landings in the region. The dates of operations were also changed to sow even more confusion. This included setting up an Arab medical conference in Beirut with the condition that it had to be finished by 16 June, then cancelled along with border closures.

The problem with deception plans is that real operations can uncover them. An Allied capture of the Italian island and airbase at Pantelleria (Operation Corkscrew) could have undone much of the work. The Barclay team worked hard to provide a cover plan.[23] Similarly, Eisenhower's plan to move his headquarters to Malta, caused the deception planners sleepless nights.

The most successful intelligence plan was Operation Mincemeat.[24] This involved floating the corpse of William Martin, a Royal Marine officer (actually Glyndwr Michael, a tramp who died of rat poison) off the coast of Spain with fake plans for the invasion of Greece and Sardinia, with Sicily as a feint. The covering letter was a clever blend of the personal and army politics, which also expressed concern about the build-up of German forces in Greece. The Spanish Government shared the papers with the Abwehr, which ended up on Hitler's desk. Ultra-decrypts showed that the Germans fell for the ruse and OKW continued to give priority to the defence of Greece. The story formed the basis of the 1956 film '*The Man Who Never Was*' and a new version, '*Operation Mincemeat*', starring Colin Firth was released in 2022.

Operation Barclay was largely successful, not least because it played into Hitler's fears that the Balkans represented his weak flank. He ordered an increase of German forces in the Balkans from 8 to 18 divisions, despite an OKW assessment that Sicily would be the next Allied target. The Abwehr prepared for the destruction of installations and planting 'stay-behind' agents. Rommel was to be appointed as commander of Army Group B in Salonika to direct anti-invasion operations should the Allies attack through the Balkans.[25] On 25 July, he landed in Salonika on an inspection of Greece's defences. However, he remained there for only one day before being recalled to Hitler's headquarters after Mussolini had been arrested.

### The Italian Collapse

The fall of Mussolini on 25 July 1943 and his replacement by Marshal Badoglio did not immediately take Italy out of the war. The new Italian foreign minister, Guariglia, was the ambassador to Turkey and time was lost while waiting for his return from Ankara. However, even after that, the new government did not attempt to contact the Allies or defend the country from German troops entering the country. When negotiations were started, the new government dithered and unrealistically asked the Turkish government to mediate. They only agreed to an armistice after an ultimatum from General Eisenhower. By this time, the Germans were ready, taking control of key positions and disarming Italian troops. They also rescued Mussolini and established the Fascist Republic of Salò on Lake Garda.

Whilst the Germans moved quickly to disarm the Italian army, there were no Germans at Spezia and Taranto, the main Italian naval bases. The fleet sailed south to join the British but was attacked by German aircraft and a number of ships were sunk. Five battleships, eight cruisers, seven destroyers and many smaller ships escaped to join the Allied fleet. The Germans plugged some of the naval gap left by the Italians. U-Boats played a growing role with S-Boats and a wide range of small ships ferrying troops and supplies around the Aegean. They also used former Italian warships after the Armistice. During the war, 40 percent of all large warship losses the Germans suffered, occurred in the Mediterranean and they accounted for 57 percent of Allied losses.

Mussolini's demise did not result in any change in the Turkish diplomatic position, much to the surprise of the British. They did welcome the removal of a competitor in the Mediterranean, strengthening their position to recover the Dodecanese. It also weakened the prospects of an Axis invasion of Turkey. Informal approaches to the Germans reinforced Turkish claims to border rectifications in Bulgaria and deepened coastal defences with islands in the Aegean and Dodecanese. Ribbentrop resisted the suggestion that Turkish occupation of the Dodecanese would relieve the Germans of occupation duties, on the basis that Germany would honour the legal rights of Mussolini.

Papen argued with Ribbentrop that a deal with Turkey could bring them into the war against the Soviet Union. At the very least, the threat could result in the Soviets reaching a separate peace with the Axis. In June 1943, Molotov and Ribbentrop had held secret negotiations and while they broke down, a Turkish intervention could have revitalised them. Papen also found out that the British and Americans had rebuffed Soviet feelers about occupying parts of eastern Turkey and naval bases in the Mediterranean. He argued that concessions to Turkey could split the Allies. Despite Stalingrad, a Soviet victory was far from certain in the summer of 1943 and arguably Germany lost an opportunity to split the Allied war effort irretrievably.

Churchill was quick to send his thoughts on the fall of Mussolini to Roosevelt the day after, on 26 July. Point 11 in his memo emphasised the importance of using this opportunity to put more pressure on Turkey to join the war. However, by September, in an exchange with Field Marshall Smuts, he appeared to have softened his view, arguing that an approach to Turkey might be made later in the year. At present, he felt that Allied forces could be more usefully employed in the central Mediterranean.[26]

### Bulgaria

The death of King Boris of Bulgaria on 28 August 1943, encouraged the Turks to test the water with the Axis over Turkish claims in Bulgaria, under the auspices of a policing role. The idea being that Soviet or Allied troops might not eject them after the war. Some in Bulgaria even believed that a Turkish invasion was imminent and Bulgaria was in no position to resist.[27] At the Moscow conference (see below) the Soviets assured Turkey that they would declare war against Bulgaria if they invaded Turkey. Given Turkish concerns about the Soviet Union's post-war plans for the Balkans, this was hardly reassuring.

The Bulgarian armed forces were not involved in any major military actions other than occupation duties in northeast Greece, Macedonia and Serbia. The 16th Infantry Division provided coastal defence on the Aegean coast. The rest of the army was deployed facing Turkey in Thrace. Bulgaria was low on the German list of equipment priorities because it was not fighting in Russia. It did acquire a range of surplus artillery, including 400 Skoda 37mm anti-tank guns and over 200 French and Belgium 75mm, 105mm and 150mm howitzers.[28] The real shortage was for motor vehicles, as a Bulgarian infantry division typically only had 40 to 50 but only a small number could be funded from the budget. Bulgaria was planning for a defensive war against Turkey, so artillery was the priority.

The army retained a cavalry (quick) division as even the Germans thought these were useful in the Balkan terrain. This did not stop the modest development of armoured forces with the establishment of an armoured regiment in June 1941, which consisted of all 98 Bulgarian tanks, plus motorised infantry and artillery. The main tanks were Skoda, Vickers and

The Germans supplied the StuG III assault gun to Bulgaria. (Photo by Author, Belgrade Kalemegdan)

Renault R35s, all hopelessly outdated by the end of 1942. As German units withdrew from the Balkans, the Bulgarians undertook additional occupation duties, which required an increase in motor vehicles with an infantry division having 173 (in theory, if not in practice).

In early 1943 the Bulgarians entered into discussions with the Germans for new equipment to respond to Operation Gertrud, potential Allied landings in Greece and Turkey entering the war. They estimated that Turkey had 24 divisions in Thrace and reserves at Istanbul and would need modern weapons if they were to participate in an attack in Thrace to control the Straits. In total, they requested 52 assault guns, 140 light tanks, 72 medium tanks, 186 armoured troop carriers and 138 armoured cars, as well as thousands of trucks, engineer vehicles and motor cycles.[29] The Germans were not in a position to supply equipment on this scale even if they wanted to. In February 1943, they offered to equip an armoured brigade with 20 StuG III, 12 Panzer IV and 20 armoured cars (Sd.Kfz.222 and 223).

This was expanded to 25 StuG III and 43 Panzer IVs in what became known as Plan 43. A few Pkw 38(t), H39 and S35 tanks were provided for training purposes at the combat school based in Nis. The actual delivery was slow and the Panzer IV variants were G and H models, ironically similar to those supplied to Turkey. By the late summer of 1943, the armoured brigade had 56 Panzer IVs and a further 27 were delivered by the end of the year. They also had 55 StuG IIIG by January 1944, which were deployed in a separate Assault Gun Detachment. Anti-tank battalions were also reorganised on the German model equipped with 404 50mm Pak38 L/60 and 180 75mm Pak40 L/46 anti-tank guns. They were all motorised with a variety of tractors by 1944. Infantry divisions also received 52,000 rifles, 7,700 sub-machine guns, 1800 80mm mortars and over 5,000 MG34 machine guns, as well as nearly 200 105mm howitzers. Anti-aircraft defences were bolstered with 84 88mm, 36 20mm and 9 37mm anti-aircraft guns. A small number were motorised to support the armoured brigade.

The Bulgarian Air Force also modernised during this period. It had reorganised front line fighter and bomber units by September 1942 into Air Escadra (Air Group) with an army, bomber and fighter Polk. However, the only planes delivered in 1942 were 12 Arado Ar 196 floatplanes for patrol missions in the Black Sea. After the first Allied bomber attacks on Ploesti, the Germans recognised the value of intercepting these attacks in Bulgaria. There was also the risk of Allied invasion and the potential for Operation Gertrud.

The Bulgarian War Minister, Lieutenant General Mikhov, asked Hitler for 157 combat aircraft and questioned the delivery of Fw 190 fighters to Turkey. They contracted for 16 Me 109G in February 1942, the most advanced German fighter available for export. These were supplemented by less modern French Bloch MB 152 (20) and Dewoitine D520 fighters (100 supplied in August 1943).[30] Whilst outdated by 1943 standards, the D520 was a decent air defence fighter able to combat all types of Allied aircraft. Between November 1943 and September 1944, they had 14 confirmed kills. Some 30 second-hand ME 109s were also delivered in 1943. The air force also received 12 Ju87 Stukas and 12 Do 17 bombers, as well as 18 Fw 189 reconnaissance aircraft. A radar system was established in 1943, which improved the air defence response as the Allies added Sofia to its list of targets in late 1943 and early 1944. It was these raids that resulted in Liberator bombers force landing in Turkey. One Liberator, known as 'Hadley's Harem', had to crash land off the Turkish coast near Manavgat. The surviving crew swam to the shore and were helped by villagers. They were declared 'shipwrecked mariners' allowing them to avoid internment. The plane has since, been recovered and the remains can be seen today at the Rahmi M. Koc Museum in Istanbul.

In 1944, a further 28 second-hand Me 109G fighters were supplied with another 13 Stukas. Bulgarian bombers also saw action in support of their occupation forces in Yugoslavia.

While generally on the defensive in December 1943, the Germans almost implemented Operation Gertrud, the invasion of Turkey. The Bulgarian Army in Thrace consisted of 10 infantry divisions, one cavalry division and one armoured brigade, all equipped with the modern weapons listed earlier. The Germans planned to support the Bulgarians with the 4th SS-Polizei Panzergrenadier Division and around nine regimental or battalion sized units of assault guns and artillery. A Gebirgsjäger and two Jager divisions would form a second line. Operation Gertrud was called off in January 1944 after the invasion of Italy and other than anti-partisan operations, the Bulgarian Army took no part in combat operations until September 1944. However, the German rearming of Bulgaria did give the Turks another reason to deflect Churchill's concept of a Balkan offensive. The reverse threat also worked for the Bulgarians, as Hitler did not press them too hard to provide divisions on the eastern front.

**Operation Accolade – the Dodecanese**

As the name implies, the Dodecanese consist of 12 islands—Nisyros, Cos, Kasos, Patmos, Calchi, Leros, Tilos, Simi, Stampalia, Lipsos, Scarpanto and Kalymnos. Rhodes and Casteloriso are generally recognised as being part of this group as well. From the sixteenth century, the islands had been under Turkish rule, although most of the population were Greek. They remained in Turkish hands until

The Germans supplied large numbers of captured French Dewoitine D.520 to the Bulgarian Air Force. Although dated by 1943 standards it was still an effective fighter when intercepting Allied bombers. (Photo by Roland Turner)

the Italo-Turkish War of 1911–1912, when the Italians seized them to cut off supplies to the main theatre of war in Libya. Despite a treaty obligation to hand them back, the various conflicts between 1912 and 1923 meant that the Italians held on to the islands. Neither Turkey nor Greece pretended to enjoy the Italian occupation of the Dodecanese but each regarded the taking over of these islands by the other as an equal threat. There were Italian garrisons on most of the islands and a German division and aircraft on the biggest island Rhodes with its harbours and airfields.

After the Adana conference, plans for an attack in the eastern Mediterranean were not high on General Wilson's strategic priorities, coming fourth after aid for Turkey. However, he had significant numbers of combat troops, totalling some 267,000 men, available for operations. The challenge was the shortage of landing craft and aircraft carriers, which dogged all Allied plans in Europe and the Far East. He nevertheless started to plan operations against the Dodecanese, Crete and even mainland Greece in case opportunities arose. The British had been active around the islands for some time using small boats of the Levant Schooner Flotilla, based in Beirut.[31]

Churchill was keen to keep these options open and in a note to Roosevelt on 5 April 1943, said that if operations against the Italian mainland were not practical, 'in that case we must be ready for an attack on the Dodecanese for supporting Turkey if she gets into trouble'. The planners argued that this would increase the threat to the Balkans, including Germany's economic needs and open up the port of Izmir to enable Turkey to join the war. General Wilson viewed his plans for Operation Accolade as a prelude to major operations, 'based on Istanbul and Salonika with objectives up to the line of the Danube'. While this may appear to be fanciful, it was considered in the context of a possible Italian collapse and growing resistance operations in the Balkans, particularly in Yugoslavia and Greece. According to the Joint Planning Staff these movements could be supported by developing a bridgehead at Durazzo in Albania and they even considered a plan to seize the Ploesti oilfields by air.[32]

As noted above, the Americans were not convinced and viewed operations in the Eastern Mediterranean as a distraction from both the Italian campaign and, more importantly, Overlord. They reiterated this at the Washington Conference in May 1943. Even the British Chiefs of Staff thought Greece was a step too far, not that Churchill agreed with them. Either way, the British were on their own in the eastern Mediterranean. Ironically, Hitler and Churchill agreed on the strategic importance of the islands. Faced with the prospect that Italy might soon be unable to carry on the war, Hitler declared that the Italian peninsula could be sealed off but they must hold the Balkans for its raw materials and to ensure German security.[33]

Approaches were made to Turkey for assistance with harbours for the Royal Navy, air bases and even Turkish participation in the landings themselves. Although British commanders were sceptical of the benefits Turkish airfields would bring, given the absence of radar early warning systems. While the Turks rejected these requests, the German refusal to hand over the islands to Turkey after the Italian collapse resulted in some low-level support from Turkey. In particular, they helped with the evacuation of British troops, with Bodrum becoming an important recovery port. Turkish troops went as far as taking troops who landed on the coast to the British Consul at Bodrum, who compensated Greek fishermen.[34] In a note to Roosevelt, Churchill said, 'Internment in Turkey is not strict and may not last long; or they may get out along the Turkish coast'.[35] The Royal Navy also withdrew to Turkish waters during the day before sortieing out at night. However, the slow pace of negotiations with the Turks resulted in Accolade moving ahead in the priorities above Operation Hardihood support to the Turks.

The Italian collapse resulted in urgent missives from Churchill to Middle East Command for immediate action, including the seizure of Rhodes. Eisenhower was concerned at the diversion of landing craft and aircraft, arguing that Accolade should be abandoned.[36] Churchill recounted that this was the most acute difference he had with Eisenhower during the war. Meanwhile, the Germans had been prepared for this eventuality with Operation Axis. They had nine divisions in the region – one Gebirgsjäger (mountain) division in the Epirus area, one division at Salonika, one division at Larissa, the 104th Infantry Division at Agrinio, the 11th Infantry Division at Piraeus, the 117th Infantry Division and one armoured division in the Peloponnese, the 22nd Infantry Division on Crete. The Kriegsmarine also had four coastal defence flotillas in the Aegean, including bases at Crete and Lemnos. These were mostly requisitioned vessels fitted with anti-aircraft weapons.

Sturm Division Rhodos had four motorised infantry battalions, a tank battalion, divisional artillery and support troops. They also garrisoned Scarpanto with a 1,500 strong fortress battalion. These forces quickly disarmed the Italian troops with only a few resisting, despite attempts by a British liaison group, including Major, the Earl Jellico, to persuade the Italian garrison commander to come over to the Allies.[37] Admiral Donitz recommended that the Germans evacuate the islands but Hitler refused, concerned that it would weaken Germany's standing with Turkey.[38]

In May, the initial British invasion plan required three infantry divisions, one armoured brigade, two independent infantry battalions, two parachute battalions and support units. The critical problem was the provision of air cover for the landing of these forces some 250 miles from the nearest British airfields in Cyprus. The Accolade Air Plan envisaged 35 RAF squadrons and 43 American squadrons for the operation.[39] Such a force was not available in September and in any case, the landing craft were not available. This did not deter Churchill from urging the landing of troops from *caiques* (Greek fishing boats) and ships' boats, 'I hope the Staffs will be able to stimulate action, which may gain immense prizes at little cost, though not at little risk'. And later, he telegraphed General Wilson with typical Churchillian rhetoric, 'This is a time to think of Clive and Peterborough and of Rooke's men taking Gibraltar'.

No amount of rhetoric was going to substitute for the hard-military facts that Wilson simply did not have the resources to attack Rhodes. Therefore, smaller operations were planned for Kos and Leros in September 1943. Kos stood only a mile off the Turkish coast and had a harbour and a small airfield. South African Air Force Spitfires flew into Kos along with 120 paras and secured the support of the Italian garrison. The main body of troops, a battalion of the Durham Light Infantry, sailed in. Luftwaffe attacks rendered the airfield unusable,[40] and a brigade group of German forces landed on 3 October. In three days of fighting, they captured the island taking 900 Allied and 3,000 Italian troops prisoners.

Leros had a port and not much else, although the coastal gun batteries guarding the sea entrances inspired Alistair Maclean's novel and later film, *The Guns of Navarone*. The Italian garrison numbered 5,500 men but only a battalion were combat troops, mostly elderly reservists and poorly equipped. The British landed three battalions who quickly came under heavy bombardment from the Luftwaffe. On 12 November, a German invasion force landed, supported by a parachute landing of 500 men, which disrupted already poor British communications. After fierce fighting, the British commander

Leros war cemetery. (Tom Oates, CC BY-SA 3.0)

surrendered the island on 16 November with 4,600 prisoners. Two other island garrisons, Samos and Castelrosso, were also evacuated.

The Leros campaign was a disaster. An expedition that could not be effectively reinforced by sea or protected from the air was doomed to failure. The nearest air bases were 450 miles away in Alexandria and 250 miles away in Cyprus and warships had to return to base to refuel after two nights in Aegean at the most. Other failures included inadequate AA guns, unjustified assumptions of Italian support and poor communications. The fortress commander, Tilney, was an artillery officer with no experience in infantry warfare. His strategy of defending the island perimeter was too ambitious for the limited number of troops at his disposal.

The British failed in the Dodecanese because they had failed to learn the lessons of Norway and Malaya. It was simply not possible to maintain garrisons where the enemy has control of the air. In addition, the operation was ill-prepared and should have been called off once the Germans seized Rhodes. Anthony Rogers, in his study of the campaign, concluded that this campaign was a reckless gamble with the lives of troops and Churchill lost.[41] It was also a major defeat for the Allied navies, which lost eight destroyers, two submarines and 10 smaller ships. A further five cruisers and four destroyers were seriously damaged. Donitz also began to appreciate the strategic value of the Aegean, arguing that a submarine base at Lemnos could control access to the Dardanelles.

The British CIGS Alan Brooke, not always a supporter of Churchill's initiatives, still believed the Allies had missed a strategic opportunity. He said, 'How different the war might be. We should have had the whole Balkans ablaze by now and the war might have finished in 1943'. It is hard to see how Brooke could sustain such an argument, so it is not difficult to see why the Americans were not convinced.

The failure of Churchill's plans in the Dodecanese was also very damaging for his efforts to get Turkey into the war. It was a clear message that the Germans could inflict serious damage to Turkish towns on the south coast. Consulate officials reported the arrival of British troops in Bodrum, fleeing the Kos battles, created a very bad impression on Turkish opinion. As Churchill himself noted in his history of the war,[42] the Turks became less helpful due to this failure. At least he did not blame General Wilson, accepting that he had done his best with 'such small bits and pieces as were left to you. Nil desperandum'.

## Moscow to Tehran Conferences

The Allied foreign ministers met in Moscow on 19 October 1943. The Russian foreign minister Molotov argued that Turkish neutrality favoured Germany and they needed to be brought into the war. While this may have been music to Churchill's ears and helped bring pressure on the Americans, it simply reinforced Turkish concerns about the intentions of the Soviet Union.

The Moscow conference's outcome was that Turkey would be asked to come in before the end of 1943 and provide air bases immediately. The Americans only agreed because it did not commit them to provide additional resources. Churchill, in a memo to Eden in Moscow, urged him to test the Soviets further on Turkey. If Turkey entered the war, that would open the Straits to the Royal Navy currently operating in the Aegean. He, therefore, sought the Soviet view of British naval forces operating in the Black Sea, supporting their advance into the Balkans. However, even in 1943, Churchill recognised that the Soviets might not want Britain to develop a large scale Balkan strategy for political reasons.

After Moscow, Eden met Menemencioğlu in Cairo on 5–7 November. Menemencioğlu claimed that Eden told him Turkey had to declare war within a month due to Soviet insistence. The threat was the unenviable position Turkey would be in with regards to the Soviets. Eden's record conflicts with this, stating that he spoke primarily about air bases. In the Turkish view, air bases meant entering the war as RAF squadrons in the Straits would bring a German response. It would be surprising if Eden went as far as Menemencioğlu claimed, given that even Churchill, in his communication to Eden in Moscow, accepted that Britain could not support Turkey with enough air support due to commitments in Italy. He hoped Turkey would enter the war in phases on their own initiative.

Irrespective of the Cairo spat, Turkey moved on 17 November ,with a private declaration that Turkey would enter the war in principle. This followed a somewhat heated, nine and a half-hour debate of the governing party's parliamentary group. However, they still refused access to the bases and required an overall plan before fixing a date for full participation. At this stage, the Turks also knew that the Americans were opposed to Churchill's Balkan approach.

The Tehran conference on 29 November was the first of the big Allied strategy conferences that included the leaders of Britain, the USA and the Soviet Union. The main focus was on plans for the invasion of France (Operation Overlord). However, Turkey was also discussed in detail and it was agreed that it would be desirable if Turkey came into war on the side of the Allies before the end of the year. The Soviets, despite their position at the Moscow conference did not press this issue, which as usual, was led by Churchill. They probably viewed Allied involvement in the Balkans as impeding their plans and were less keen on a militarily stronger Turkey on their doorstep. Roosevelt was also unenthusiastic, wanting to focus on Overlord, a priority supported by Stalin. Churchill believed that he could have won Stalin round to his view on Turkey but for the influence of American military advisers on Roosevelt.[43] He also reflected on the British experience in training Turkish troops, highlighting the poor attendance at military schools and that they were not quick to learn.

Churchill brought the Soviets closer to his position by suggesting that if the Turks did not enter the war, this would have consequences regarding to the future status of the Straits. A point picked up in later Soviet demands on Turkey. For now, Stalin argued that even Churchill's modest estimate of two or three divisions, 20 air squadrons and flak units were an unnecessary diversion from Overlord. However, he was still in favour of bringing Turkey into the war and recognised the value of seizing islands in the Aegean. He also said that the Soviet Union would declare war on Bulgaria if they threatened Turkey with the Germans.

### Cairo Conference 4–7 December 1943

What is known as the Second Cairo Conference, was held on 4–6 December 1943, to address Turkey's possible contribution to the Allies as agreed at Tehran. Roosevelt, Churchill and İnönü attended the meeting. The Turkish spin before the meeting indicated that there was significant internal opposition to Turkey entering the war, which could threaten İnönü's position as President. The British Foreign Office regarded this as unlikely, given İnönü's grip on the government and the press.

Churchill played the Soviet card during the conference while İnönü emphasised the danger of Turkey entering the war unprepared. He argued that the equipment promised at Adana had not all been delivered. Churchill countered by pointing to Turkey's limited capacity and inability to use the equipment already provided, properly. Roosevelt was concerned that US equipment to Turkey would weaken Overlord but Churchill persuaded him that there was no requirement for US weaponry. On this basis, Roosevelt did press İnönü with the threat that Turkey would need allies after the war. He confirmed that 15 February 1944 was the critical date for Turkish entry into the war. Churchill drafted a memorandum to the British Chiefs of Staff on 6 December, setting out the actions necessary if Turkey entered the war (Operation Saturn).[44] This included the preparation and protection of Turkish airfields, bombing of enemy airfields to cover the fighter fly-in to Turkey and six to eight submarines based at Ismet for operations in the Black Sea.

On his return from Cairo, İnönü asked Marshal Çakmak for a report on the preparedness of Turkish armed forces. He painted a grim picture with only one-third of aircraft operational and the anti-aircraft guns with poorly trained crews. This at least confirms the British Colonel Sleeman's report. When the official answer was given on 12 December that Turkish forces would not be ready by 15 February 1944, this led to a string of rancorous exchanges between Britain and Turkey. Churchill told Eden that Turkish claims of a

President Roosevelt, President İnönü, Prime Minister Winston Churchill and aides, including Anthony Eden at the Second Cairo Conference in December 1943. (US Army Signal Corps)

German invasion were 'absolute rubbish' and their failure to meet the 15 February deadline would be the virtual end of the alliance with Turkey.

### Operation Hercules

Linked to the Cairo conference was a British plan for the combined British and Turkish capture of the German-occupied island of Rhodes, an undertaking proposed to Turkey as an inducement for that country's entry into the war with another attempt to break German strength in the Aegean during the winter of 1943–1944. This was also viewed as an effort to distract the Germans from Overlord. The plan was to use 4th Division and the Gibraltar Brigade for the operation together with support troops.

British intelligence assessed the Turkish army strength at this time as being 39 infantry divisions, four mountain divisions, three cavalry divisions and one armoured brigade. However, there remained concerns about the over-centralised leadership and poor infrastructure. A report stated that 'Initiative on the part of even quite senior generals, is neither taught nor encouraged in peace and it is inconceivable that it will suddenly blossom in war'. They assessed that small arms would be handled well by what they regarded as tough well-disciplined troops but training in new weapons is elementary in the extreme. In particular, the principles of anti-tank defence had not filtered through to infantry divisions, which would result in weapons being handled bravely but unscientifically. This shows that Marshal Çakmak's assessment of his forces to the Turkish political leadership was shared by the British.

Planning included another round of discussion about equipment and airfield access. The Turkish military sought huge amounts of equipment, including 216 Spitfires, 500 Sherman tanks, 550 pieces of artillery, 1000 anti-tank guns and 7000 lorries. A memo to Eisenhower sets out the British understanding of the Cairo conference agreement,[45] which included the infiltration from Syria of 250 specialists (Force 686), mostly RAF, to prepare air bases for Allied squadrons. It also states that if there was not a positive response, 'the Allies would abandon Turkey'.

There was plenty of Allied scepticism of the plan in memos in the War Office files. This was based on experience of dealing with the Turks and resource limitations. As one report put it, 'We cannot emphasise too strongly that past experience of the Turks indicates that it is impossible to run any programme with any degree of reliance that it can be fulfilled'. There was no expectation that the Germans would attempt a land attack on Turkey, although the British military assessment was that it would force them to shift four or five divisions to bolster Bulgaria.[46] The Germans could shift around 150 bombers and 75 dive-bombers to the region quickly, putting the new Turkish airbases at risk. The Allied plan was for the Turkish army to maintain light forces on the border while holding the Catalja and Bulair lines in strength. There were no planned offensive operations against Bulgaria, although there was scope for small scale seaborne operations in the Aegean. Allied forces would strengthen the airfield defences with seven RAF squadrons (the Turks wanted 49 squadrons) and AA units and capture Rhodes to open up the Aegean to shipping. In preparation for these actions, some 2000 Allied personnel would be infiltrated into Turkey before 15 February, with a further 3000 afterwards. The main route for troops and stores would be the rail routes using nine trains every day.

The plan was cancelled in February 1944, just one month before its scheduled implementation, due to the Turkish response to the proposal at Cairo for them to enter the war on 15 February.

Şükrü Âli Ögel, Director of the highly regarded Turkish intelligence service the MAH until July 1941. (via William Cobb)

### Intelligence Operations

Turkey was an important battlefield in the intelligence war between the Axis and the Allies in the Second World War. Turkey's non-belligerency allowed the combatants to maintain diplomatic missions and work under diplomatic cover on intelligence operations. This was a period when all sides stepped up their intelligence operations in and around Turkey. Istanbul and Ankara were the crucibles of a secret war where nations spied and subverted each other. The main protagonists were the Abwehr, the German Intelligence Service and the British Secret Intelligence Service (SIS). Other agencies, including the Gestapo for the Germans and SOE for the British, also operated in Turkey.

The Turkish National Security Service (*Milli Emniyet Hizmeti*, MEH but known as MAH) was created by Atatürk in 1926 and reported to the Ministry of the Interior. The first director was Şükrü Âli Ögel, who had served as a staff officer during the War of Independence. He retired from the army as a colonel in 1936 but remained as the director of MAH. Perhaps more unusually, he became a deputy in the Turkish Grand National Assembly in 1937 yet remained in post at MAH until a falling out with Prime Minister Refik Saydam in July 1941. He was replaced by Mehmet Naci Perkel, who had been captured by the British in the First World War at the Battle of Kut al-Amara and spent five years in prisoner of war camps in India before his release in 1920. He joined MAH in 1929 as a Staff Major and was appointed Deputy Director in 1934.

The MAH kept a close watch on all the foreign intelligence service operations in Turkey. While the British viewed the Turkish state and military as uniformly inefficient, they regarded the secret service as thorough and effective. MAH aided both sides as Turkish policy flowed during the war, although they strongly favoured the British. As we have seen, the Royal Navy was allowed to use Turkish territorial waters and Allied military transport was allowed to fly over the Turkish coast. Less well known is a collaboration with the Germans to send German-trained agents into Russia from Turkey. These were Georgians, Caucasians, Azerbaijanis and Turks. The understanding was that when they obtained information that concerned the Turks, the Germans would pass it on.[47] The MAH would act when the Germans acted against non-Soviet targets. For

Brigadier Dudley Clarke head of 'A Force', which was responsible for intelligence work in Turkey. (Artwork by Patrick Edward Phillips)

example, In April 1941, the Turks picked up a German agent alleged to be engaged in operations against Allied shipping from Greek and Turkish ports.

The British had a range of intelligence operations in Turkey, with the old embassy building in Istanbul an important base. They also used embassy officials in Ankara like other nations. Churchill had sent Admiral Howard Kelly to Turkey, who built up a good relationship with Turkish officers, including Marshall Çakmak, despite being frequently arrested for going on walks near strategic installations. He reported that Turkey had no intention of going to war in 1940 but Churchill ignored his view.

The more aggressive activities (primarily SOE) were discouraged by the British Ambassador but the SIS had more leeway. As far back as 1938, Colonel Lawrence Grand had been appointed to establish the Devices and Destruction Section of MI6 (Section D), camouflaged with the title Statistical Research Department. Grand established a network of agents, particularly in the Balkans. Security Intelligence Middle East (SIME) was responsible for security and counterintelligence in the Middle East, led by Brigadier R.J. Maunsell. This was part of a wider Middle East operation led by Brigadier Dudley Clarke. Relations with the MAH have been described as cordial, if not quite a special relationship, and they gave the British considerable assistance.[48]

President İnönü ordered his secret service to work with the British at the expense of the Germans. In November 1940, SIME and the Turkish service founded the Anglo-Turkish Security Bureau, funded by the former and administered by the latter. The British were able to run a number of double agents whose tasks included deception operations, of which *Cheese* based in Cairo, was particularly successful once Axis agents had been captured. It was through Turkey that the Abwehr was fed most misinformation about operations. Some of the most effective agents were the Taurus Express attendants in the sleeping cars because this was the only method of travelling between Istanbul and the Arab states. In addition to the usual embassy operations under cover of commercial interests, SOE used the Goeland Shipping Company and the Anglo-Danubian Transport & Trading Corporation, as fronts for intelligence and sabotage operations.[49]

The British also had access to codebreaking facilities (including Ultra and diplomatic decrypts) which allowed them to track German activity and monitor the Turks. This also confirmed that Turkish intelligence aid to the Germans was not comparable with that afforded to the British. While Ultra has been given a lot of attention in recent years, we should not forget the diplomatic decrypts, which Churchill paid much attention to. Robin Dennison's study of these about Turkey is interesting, but as he concludes, they do not result in any significant rewriting of history.[50] They also provide the reader with some broad context for their wartime decisions but the decrypts were generally not useful for instant tactical decisions.

Britain also mounted a propaganda effort early in the war. Sir Denison Ross, formerly Director of the University of London's School of Oriental Studies, arrived in early 1940 to establish a British Information Office in Istanbul. However, the effort was not on the same scale as the Germans and coordination between different ministries was poor.[51] Efforts were made to improve this in 1941 and by 1943 a joint plan was agreed to support efforts to get Turkey into the war. This included improving the availability of British publications and financing Turkish ones. The BBC Turkish Service was broadcast four times a day with several different types of programmes. However, they resisted attempts to include propaganda messages, sticking to its tradition of straight news.

Germany's main overseas secret service was the Abwehr, whose station in Turkey was in Istanbul (later moved to Ankara). Abwehr stations operated under diplomatic or commercial fronts and were called *Kriegsorganisationen* (Kos). Outstations, called *Nebenstallen*, included Tehran, Istanbul, Kabul and smaller units in Adana, Iskenderun and Antakya. They also had related operations in Lebanon, Athens and Sofia, which the British called 'The Balkan Watchtower'. By March 1944, about 36–40 officials worked for German intelligence organisations in Turkey and had an extensive network of Turkish contacts.[52]

The Abwehr had a poor reputation as an intelligence service, not helped by the British breaking their cyphers, which was the primary means of communication between Ankara and Berlin. Another weakness was the inadequate evaluation of intelligence at OKW and in the Abwehr.[53] There was, what we would call today, 'information overload' with too much 'noise' to be able to identify what was really important. So much so that British deception plans often did not cut through the chatter, although that changed as radio interception and air reconnaissance sources dried up. It was also undermined by the internal political intrigues and competition with other agencies, particularly the SS. Paul Leverkuhn, the station chief in Istanbul, argued that the weakness of the German intelligence system, was the way in which intelligence was evaluated and used,[54] which resulted from the way the OKW was organised. Papen, in his memoirs, also referred to the uncoordinated way intelligence agencies operated.

The Abwehr and its chief Admiral Wilhelm Canaris was regarded with suspicion by the SS, who also mounted operations abroad through the Reich Security Main Office and the *Sicherheitsdienst* (SD) and wanted to take over their role. They ran their own network of agents independent of the Abwehr. Canaris had contacted British intelligence regarding peace terms. In late 1943, Paul Leverkuhn helped a known dissident, Erich Vermeeren de Saventhem, get an assignment as a junior agent in Istanbul. Vermeeren's wife was related to Papen and after some difficulties, she was able to join him there. When both were summoned back to Berlin, they decided to defect to the British, who made it look like a kidnapping, smuggling the couple out of Turkey through Aleppo.

It was wrongly believed that he absconded with Abwehr codes however, he did provide useful intelligence. Some 20 Abwehr agents fled Turkey to avoid arrest, although one, Glentschkowski, deserted to the British. He was a Russian specialist and irreplaceable, which meant the British viewed him as important as Vermehren. Hitler was furious and the case contributed to his decision to abolish the Abwehr in February 1944. Canaris was executed in April 1945 for being associated with the bomb plot to kill Hitler.

Other Nazi organisations focused on propaganda with a focus on anti-Soviet messaging after Operation Barbarossa. The Auslands-Organisation (AO) established chapters in Ankara, Istanbul and Izmir. They sponsored Nazi sympathisers to publish articles and supplied bookstores with anti-Soviet books and invited people to plays and social gatherings. Pressure was also placed on left-leaning newspapers like *Tan* through an advertising boycott and restrictions on paper, which was imported from Germany. Turkish intelligence closely monitored German publications and institutions, as well as Turkish citizens who supported these activities. Intelligence operatives were inserted into foreign news agencies for counterintelligence purposes.

The most successful German intelligence operation was Operation Cicero, which took place between October 1943 and April 1944, described by Mark Simmons as 'Hitler's most successful spy'.[55] Cicero was the code name for the British Ambassador's valet, who photographed top-secret documents that the Ambassador kept in his personal safe and document boxes. He sold them to the Germans through his handler, L.C. Moyzisch, an attaché at the German embassy, although actually a representative of the SS.

Moyzisch wrote his account of the affair in a 1950 book.[56] Cicero was paid some £300,000 for around 400 photographed documents. Some of these were very important, including partial notes of the Casablanca, Moscow, Tehran and Cairo conferences. They may also have enabled the cypher section to break elements of British codes. He also handed over a document that mentioned Operation Overlord, including the earlier planned date in May 1944. It also gave the Germans an understanding of the scale of Lend-Lease equipment being supplied to Turkey and the likelihood of Turkey entering the war. In particular, von Papen discovered that an Allied attack on the Balkans through Salonika could be ruled out, which should have led to the redeployment of German divisions to other fronts.

The Germans appear to have made limited use of this intelligence, partly because of turf wars in Berlin. Ribbentrop suspected that the documents were false, even after it was apparent they were genuine. In an annexe to Moyzisch's book, von Papen suggests that there is more to the story, although he confirms the main facts. Cicero was subsequently identified as Elyesa Bazna, an Albanian who wrote his own account in 1962. He was never caught by the British, leaving the embassy in April 1944 when the British recognised it was the embassy that was the source of the leaks. He lived in Turkey after the war and later moved to Munich. He died in Germany in 1970, aged 66.

They say treachery never pays and in this case, they may be right. Most of the money he was paid was in counterfeit Sterling and he spent a short time in a Turkish prison as a consequence. He tried, unsuccessfully, to get the West German government to reimburse him in the 1960s. The film based on the story, *5 Fingers*, was released in 1952 and Bazna, renamed Ulysses Diello, was played by James Mason. It was nominated for an academy award but despite being

Elyesa Bazna, Agent Cicero. (Public Domain)

described as a true story, it takes huge liberties with the facts and large parts are fiction. More recently, there is a 2019 Turkish take on the story, *Operation Cicero,* directed by Serdar Akar.

Less successful was Operation François, an attempt made by the Abwehr to use the Qashqai people in Iran to sabotage British and American supplies bound for the Soviet Union. After German nationals had been expelled from Iran (Operation Countenance), two intelligence officers remained as stay-behind agents. Operation François was one of 14 plans in 1943, of which only three were carried out. It was led by Otto Skorzeny, who sent elements of the 502nd SS Jager Battalion to parachute into Iran during the summer of 1943. Skorzeny remained behind to train more recruits but regarded the operation as a failure mainly due to inadequate reinforcements and supplies.

Others argue that again, it was inter-service rivalry that undermined operations and an effective response from British intelligence in Iran.[57] Turkey was the only relatively safe route the Germans had to insert agents into the Middle East, as parachuting was risky. Even so, many were intercepted and those that did get through had radios that did not reach outstations in Turkey. A special Luftwaffe squadron (Gartenfeld) was attached to the Abwehr for this type of operation using four-engine Focke-Wulf Fw 200 Condor and from 1942 onwards, the Junkers Ju 290, which could fly at high altitude undetected over Turkey.

The Germans had several sabotage plans (Operation Mammut 1-3) using the Kurds, promising an independent Kurdistan based primarily on land in Iraq and Iran. Papen opposed any spill-over into Turkey as this would upset the Turks. They built up links with the Kurdish Sheik Mahmoud but attempts to insert German liaison teams failed.

The Italians had a limited range of intelligence operations in the region, relying heavily on diplomatic sources and some individuals. The MAH paid particular attention to Italians given the fragile diplomatic relations, despite occasional thaws in relations during the period 1928–1932.

The Americans posted George Earle – their former envoy to Bulgaria – as a naval attaché to Istanbul. He was tasked with improving relations between Bulgaria and Turkey and he also cooperated with similar anti-Axis efforts in Hungary. The Turks viewed these efforts as a Balkan bulwark against the Soviets. However, the Germans saw the risk that the Balkan states could make a separate peace with the USA. Papen's failure to recognise this risk further undermined Ribbentrop's confidence in the ambassador. He had Papen's first deputy, Hans Kroll appointed to supervise intelligence work in Turkey. Increasingly, intelligence officers reported directly to Berlin.

The American intelligence services in Ankara also discovered agent Cicero from their own asset in the German embassy, Cornelia Kapp. She had lived in the USA with her diplomat father before the war and may have been recruited when working for her father in Sofia in 1943. She was described as being of a nervous disposition and was transferred from Sofia when the air raids began. She offered to work for the Americans in return for being allowed to go back to the USA. As Moyzisch's secretary, she had access to a range of secret papers that she copied. She knew of Cicero but not his real name and had spoken to him on the phone. She may even have met him by accident in an Ankara department store. She persuaded the Americans that she had been discovered and was spirited out of Turkey by them to the USA. Her defection added to the pressure on Moyzisch, who managed to avoid returning to Germany and probable arrest, before the war ended.

The Japanese had made Sofia the centre of intelligence operations in the region. Commanded by Akira Yamaji and an experienced team, they flattered the Bulgarians and gave large sums of money to charities. Their liaison man in Ankara was a Bulgarian journalist, Dimitri Dragneff. The Germans distrusted the Japanese motives and kept a close eye on them.

The Soviet Union also had significant intelligence operations in Turkey, operating from the Ankara embassy and Istanbul. The NKVD (People's Commissariat for Internal Affairs) ran overseas agents as well as the NKGB (People's Commissariat for State Security), complicated by frequent purges and reorganisations. A particularly trusted agent, codenamed 'Omeri', was based in Istanbul and is credited with being influential in formulating Stalin's view of Turkey.[58] He reported on the dangers Turkey posed to Soviet interests in the Caucasus and playing to Stalin's paranoia, said that Turkey was plotting with Trotskyites to create a Caucasian Confederation. The NKGB also reported on the work of Turkish intelligence in the Caucasus and on Turkish General Staff studies of transport links and Soviet defences in the region.

While a work of fiction, '*Sea of Spies*' by Alex Girlis is set in Istanbul in 1943, it features a British spy seeking evidence of chromium shipments from Turkey to the Skoda factory in Pilsen. While the shipments were hardly a secret, the book gives a good feel for the period.

# 8
# ENDGAME

After the February 1944 deadline was not met, British-Turkish relations fell to an all-time low. The language became less diplomatic and even Churchill was considering ending the alliance. Press and parliamentary comment during the period reflects British frustration, not just with Turkey but with neutral countries generally. The Foreign Office internal communications have been described as vitriolic,[1] but they and the Joint Chiefs of Staff acted as a restraining hand as they both wanted to keep Turkey in play. İnönü recognised the risk of drifting too far from the Allies, although as ever, the growing threat of the Soviet Union was at the forefront of Turkish concerns. Consequently, the Turkish government continued to press peace initiatives, which would keep the Soviets out of the Balkans. Weber refers to a speech by Menemencioğlu setting out the basis for such a deal,[2] reflecting the Turkish leadership's persistent wishful thinking.

Hitler was also concerned about the impact that developments on the eastern front would have on Turkey's neutrality. This was the basis for his refusal to allow General Manstein to evacuate Crimea when the Soviets cut off the land bridge.[3] Hitler was concerned about the threat Soviet bombers could pose to the Romanian oilfields and he also stressed the importance of the loss of manganese ore in the mines of Nikopol on the Dneiper. Not for the first time, he complained that his generals never consider the economic implications of their proposals.

The Red Army was getting ever closer to the Turkish border in the Balkans. By April 1944, they had liberated most of the Crimea and Sevastopol fell on 9 May. In Italy, the Allies eventually broke out of the Anzio beachhead and captured Monte Cassino, forcing the Germans to abandon Rome and form a new defensive line. On 6 June, Operation Overlord began, landing 155,000 Allied troops in France, while the Red Army's Operation Bagration destroyed the German Army Group Centre.

**Turkey's Policy Shifts**

Turkey gradually began to shift its policy in line with the changing position. Internally, there was a clampdown on the pan-Turanists, disowning various private efforts by well-connected individuals to encourage the Germans to support this policy. More importantly, there were significant shifts in Turkey's foreign policy.

Deliveries to Germany of chromite had increased in the early months of 1944. So much so that the Allies bombed the bridges and tracks that linked Turkey to Bulgaria, the main rail route for Turkish exports. They also considered economic sanctions and a blockade but concluded that would not have much impact and might drive Turkey closer to Germany. In April, Turkey notified the Allies, in response to a note of protest, that they would initially reduce shipments and then cancel them altogether. Turkey also agreed to halve the export of other strategic commodities. Menemencioğlu's explanation to the Grand National Assembly for the shift of policy was interesting. He said that Turkey's alliance with Britain was the 'nucleus and basis of our foreign policy' and therefore Turkey was not neutral.

Whilst the Allies accepted the compromise on strategic commodities, they kept up the pressure on closing the Straits to German vessels. The British argued that military transports were being allowed through and Turkish inspections were inadequate. Eden's statement in the House of Commons references 'Four K.T. vessels and eight EMS craft in all, were, during the first days of June,

CHASING THE SOFT UNDERBELLY: TURKEY AND THE SECOND WORLD WAR

Turkish Foreign Minister, Numan Menemencioğlu (on the right). (Anefo)

passed through the Straits into the Aegean'.[4] As a consequence of British representations, the Turks undertook a detailed inspection of a German EMS type ship, the *Kassel* and discovered a range of war materials. This led to intensive inspections of all German ships, effectively closing this route.

At the height of the crisis, Menemencioğlu resigned as Foreign Minister following a personal appeal from Churchill to İnönü. The British had long regarded Menemencioğlu as being pro-Axis, although in practice, his focus was on the Soviet Union. Weisband argues that his policies were supported by the rest of the Turkish leadership,[5] including İnönü and he was sacrificed to placate the British. Another adjustment was the retirement of Marshall Çakmak, the pro-German Chief of Staff. At 68, he had reached retirement age but most expected him to stay in post until the end of the war. However, İnönü decided to replace him with Kâzim Orbay, who was more sympathetic to the Allies, although he was concerned that there might be an attempted military coup.[6] Forty-seven pan-Turkists were also put on trial for sedition, although the convictions were overturned when relations with the Soviet Union deteriorated in late 1945.

The British kept up the pressure with a demand that Turkey break off diplomatic relations with Germany. The Americans supported this initiative as a step to full belligerence, although as usual, Marshall warned against any military commitments that would divert resources from north-west Europe. The Soviets regarded this as a half-hearted measure and believed that Turkey should be isolated for failing to join the war earlier. Too little too late was the view from Moscow, who wished to avoid giving Turkey any post-war preferences. On 2 August 1944, the Turkish government announced they were breaking off diplomatic relations following a vote in the Grand National Assembly. The Acting Foreign Minister Saracoğlu argued that this reflected established Turkish policy while making it

clear that this was not a declaration of war. This was a serious blow to Germany, following the decision of Sweden the previous year to prevent iron ore exports.

Churchill responded positively to this development, describing it in the House of Commons as 'This act infuses new life in the alliance'.[7] He also reflected on Turkey's military position at the outbreak of war and the current time, saying, 'The Turkish Army was by no means modern. It was very much as it had come out of the last war or series of wars. I understand plainly the feelings of military prudence which made the action of Turkey less strong when these new facts were apparent to them all of a sudden at the opening of great battles'. However, there was a sting in the tail with, 'These difficulties have, to a considerable extent, been repaired'.

## Overlord and Operation Zeppelin

The invasion of Northern France, Operation Overlord, was the focus of Allied strategy in 1944. It pulled military resources from the Mediterranean theatre into Britain, weakening the Allied effort in Italy and made new operations in the eastern Mediterranean very difficult.

As late as October 1943, Churchill was still expressing his concerns about Overlord and continued to press his Mediterranean strategy despite Allied agreement on Overlord at the Quadrant conference. This included a minute to the Chiefs of Staff asking for a staff study of the situation in the Mediterranean to take account of the growing resistance in the Balkans.[8] The British General Morgan, who was planning Overlord, began to wonder if he and his team at COSSAC had wasted their time given Churchill's theory of trying everything else before a channel assault.[9] Eisenhower's Chief of Staff, Bedell Smith, reported that Churchill was still unconvinced about Overlord and wanted to attack through the Balkans.[10] It was the Americans and Stalin's eventual opposition at the Tehran conference to the British arriving in the Balkans, that forced Churchill's hand.

Despite this focus, Turkey and the Mediterranean theatre played an important role in the Allied deception plans for Overlord. Credible threats needed to be maintained to avoid German troops being withdrawn from the Balkans to reinforce the beaches of northern France. These threats were incorporated into the cover plan for Overlord called Operation Bodyguard. The best known of these deception plans was Operation Fortitude, which aimed to divert German attention away from Normandy towards Norway (Fortitude North) and the Pas de Calais (Fortitude South). This famously involved the creation of the First US Army Group commanded by General George Patton. Using physical deception, radio traffic and double agents, they persuaded Hitler that the Pas de Calais was the likely main attack point.

Less well known are the other elements of Operation Bodyguard. These included Operation Ironside, which posed a threat to capture Bordeaux. Two Allied divisions would land on D-Day, followed up by six more coming directly from the USA. These would then break out and link up with another deception plan, Operation Vendetta, the invasion of southern France; not to be confused with planning for the real Operation Anvil, later Dragoon. There was also Operation Royal Flush and Graffham, which involved largely political overtures to neutral countries like Spain and Sweden.

One challenge was hiding veteran troops returning from the Mediterranean because their return was likely to generate local stories, homecoming parties and the like. To counter this, double agents spread stories of extended leave and cadres coming home to train new units. When this could not realistically be sustained any longer, new bogus divisions were created to replace them in the

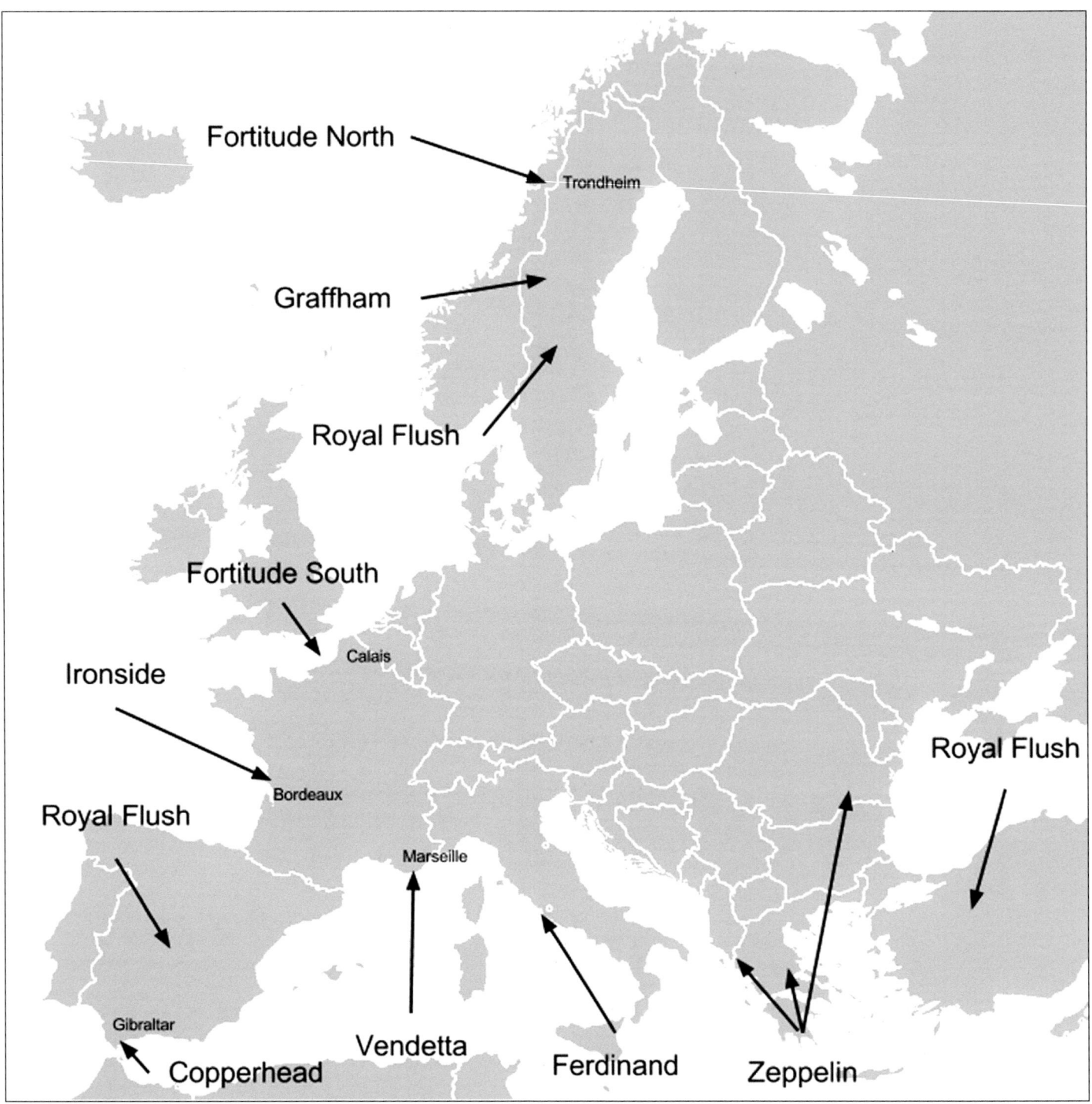

Allied deception operations in 1944. (ErrantX, CC BY-SA 3.0)

Mediterranean. The notional Allied strength in the Mediterranean grew to 70 divisions, of which a quarter were bogus.[11]

The primary deception plan in the eastern Mediterranean was Operation Zeppelin.[12] This involved developing invasion threats through Greece, Albania, Croatia, Turkey and Bulgaria. The sub-plan for an attack on Greece and Bulgaria was called Operation Turpitude. The British avoided any suggestion that Bulgaria might change sides because the Soviets wanted to achieve this without warning the Germans. The Russian General Staff agreed to assist with their part of Zeppelin, including a simulated assault against the Bulgarian and Romanian coasts. The plan envisaged four stages:

Stage 1 – To induce the enemy to make faulty strategic dispositions during early 1944.

Stages 2 and 3 – To induce him to make a false appreciation of visible offensive operations in the spring.

Stage 4 – To prevent the diversion to Northern France of enemy forces in the Mediterranean.

Operation Royal Flush also supported Zeppelin by putting political pressure on Turkey to allow Allied forces to land in Thrace to attack Greece and Bulgaria. A Foreign Office memorandum to the ambassador in Washington sets out the British strategy towards Turkey.[13] It claims the Turkish Foreign Minister had given an assurance that Turkey would enter the war, 'within one fortnight of a successful landing in the west'. The British were sceptical about this and the memo goes on to say, 'We are not, however, any longer prepared to pay any price for Turkey's entry into the war at this stage'.

The aircraft carrier HMS *Victorious* was routed through the Suez Canal as part of the Operation Zeppelin deception plan. (Public Domain)

A military mission might be sent after Overlord had been successfully concluded, although there were different views in British ministries. The Air Ministry Director of Plans said in a memorandum, 'the principle we have adopted is that if we can get a mission into the country with lots of brass hats and gold braid, the Turks and the Germans will feel that there really is something in the wind'.[14] However, the Foreign Secretary decided that such an approach would weaken British standing with the Turks. He argued that even a trickle of supplies would be hailed as a success for their policy on non-cooperation.

The selection of objectives in the detailed plan for Operation Zeppelin is as detailed as many real operations, with an order of battle that included real and bogus units. The goal of a deception operation is not to make the enemy think something; it is to make them take actions that help your plans. Even if they do not believe it is real, it is enough that the possibility means he must respond.[15] This meant the targets had to be credible. For example, Rhodes was excluded until after a notional date of Allied acquisition of ports and air bases in Turkey. Fighter cover was a major consideration as the Germans would expect the Allies to have learned the lesson of failure in the Aegean.

The practical implementation of Operation Zeppelin was coordinated by the Cairo based 'A' Force (Brigadier Dudley Clarke), under the overall command of General Wilson as Supreme Allied Commander in the Mediterranean. This involved the notional British 12th Army based in the Middle East supported by a breakout from Italy and Soviet advances into the Balkans. It included all the elements of a deception operation including, dummy units, radio traffic and intelligence agents who would plant the initial story on German intelligence and updates to explain changes in the plan at the different stages. Senior Allied commanders would be asked to visit Cairo and there would be exchange trips with Soviet officers.

Operations were undertaken on a large scale with thousands of troops involved in the latter stages, including 1000 signals personnel. It also included actual land and air raids, glider concentrations, reconnaissance flights and naval activity. The War Cabinet approved sending three large convoys totalling around 130 ships with escort carriers in support of the plan,[16] which included the fleet carrier HMS *Victorious* en route to the Far East. Hitler believed that this naval movement might increase pressure on Turkey to enter the war. The shortage of landing craft was a particular problem and the solution was to deploy dummy LCTs next to a small number of real crafts, which were moved around harbours. Effective security measures were essential and harbours at the maximum range of enemy reconnaissance were preferred.

The first threat was planned for March 1944 against Crete and Greece, which was delayed until May and then turned into Operation Turpitude during June and July. This operation envisaged an overland invasion of Greece from Turkey using Syria based forces, while units in Italy would attack Croatia and Albania (Operation Ferdinand). The Syria based units included the British Ninth Army, which was a modest force along the Turkish border and the 31st Indian Armoured Division. The fictional 20th Armoured Division (actually just a small brigade) manoeuvred real and dummy tanks along the Turkish border, which helpfully caused some concern from the Turkish command.

The plan envisaged giving Turkey an ultimatum immediately after the Russians landed at Varna in Bulgaria, demanding airfield and transit facilities. This was presumably aimed at countering German intelligence that Turkey was still unlikely to join the war. Information leaflets and maps about Thrace were printed in English by selected printing presses in the Middle East and a call went out to US forces for Turkish speakers. The Turks also became concerned when Turkish consuls at Damascus and Aleppo reported the troop movements in Syria and approached the British. Papen faithfully reported this intelligence back to Berlin, adding to Hitler's belief, widely shared in OKW, that some operation in the eastern Mediterranean was likely.

There was some evidence that the German garrisons in Greece and the islands were becoming demoralised. The garrison units were often lower quality fortress regiments, which included soldiers who were politically suspect. One example was an approach to an SOE liaison officer from a German private in the 999th Fortress regiment in the Peloponnese, who indicated that his battalion might be prepared to mutiny. He was a communist who had been a political prisoner in the Reich for five years, which demonstrated the degree to which the Germans were scraping the barrel for troops. The British response was that they were only interested in whole unit mutinies, in which units could resist German counterattacks.[17] Individual desertions would have limited benefits because the

Allies had no means of dealing with them.

These deception operations did lead the Germans to overestimate Allied troop strength in the region. They identified up to 71 divisions in early 1944, when in reality, there were only 30 divisions and OKW signals referred to the build-up of British forces in Egypt. The German High Command was not convinced the Allies would launch a major offensive in the Balkans but they did believe there would be small scale incursions, possibly including the seizure of the Ionian islands. This meant they retained their units in the Balkans, including 430 aircraft and reinforced naval forces rather than shifting units to France, thus achieving the main goals of Operation Zeppelin. Clarke regarded this operation as the swan song for 'A' Force, the party was nearly over and deception had played its part.

Crveni Krst, Nis concentration camp, southern Serbia. More than 10,000 people are thought to have been killed at the camp. (Photo by Author)

### Resistance in the Balkans

The other key element of Allied strategy in the Balkans was to tie down German units by supporting resistance groups. Turkey was less than enthusiastic about this approach, although they turned a blind eye on occasion to clandestine activities based on Turkish soil. For example, Russian and Polish deserters from the German occupation forces in Greece fighting for the resistance, were smuggled away and supplies brought in through a regular boat run between Pelion and Turkey.[18] The British Special Boat Service also made extensive use of the Turkish coast.[19] The most effective resistance groups were controlled by communist parties linked to Moscow. The Turkish government viewed a post-war Balkans dominated by the Soviet Union as a major threat.

Allied support for resistance groups was largely led by the British through the SOE based in Cairo. SOE claimed in October 1943 that there were 230,000 organised guerrillas and 80 British missions in radio contact with Cairo, pinning 17 German and eight Bulgarian divisions.[20] They used British operatives, some of whom had a pre-war knowledge of the Balkans and recruits from Balkan states. Immigrant communities in the Empire were also a useful source of native-speaking recruits. British irregular warfare advocates had significant support from the very top. Churchill had seen the effect of guerrilla warfare for himself in Cuba in 1895. He had read T.E. Lawrence's *Seven Pillars of Wisdom*, which told the story of the Arab revolt against the Ottomans in the First World War and recruited Lawrence into the Colonial Office in 1921.

The Americans, through the Office of Strategic Services (OSS), led by General Donovan, also ran operations in the Balkans, mostly from bases in Italy.[21] Donovan had toured the Balkans, including Turkey, in early 1941 before the USA had joined the war. Company C covered the Balkans with Operational Groups (OG) sent to Yugoslavia from the end of 1943. The many operations included rescuing 500 American airmen from Serbia in Operation Halyard.[22] As with the British, native-speaking migrants were often recruited for these groups. In the summer of 1943, a recruitment team had so many Greek-speaking volunteers from the 122nd Infantry Battalion that the commanding officer volunteered the whole unit. The first of these OGs landed in Greece in April 1944.[23]

In around eight months of operations, it was estimated that they had killed or wounded 1800 enemy troops and destroyed significant amounts of railway infrastructure the Germans relied upon. Interestingly, the Americans were also influenced by T.E. Lawrence. To this day, the modern US field manual on counter-insurgency cites Lawrence's 1917 guide, 'Do not try to do too much with your own hands. Better that the Arabs do it tolerably than that you do it perfectly. It is their war and you are there to help them, not to win it for them'.[24] This perfectly explains the strategy behind supporting successful resistance operations during the Second World War.

To avoid British supervision, the OSS shifted operations in Bulgaria and Romania to Istanbul under Colonel Jadwin. This led to poor cooperation and sometimes rivalry between operational teams. Most notably, in what became known as the Kuyumdjiski Affair, a claimed peace feeler from the Bulgarians to OSS in return for a halt in the bombing campaign, which came to nothing.

With the German occupation came a programme to exterminate around one and a half million Balkan Jews and other targets of their racial policies. In Romania, this was carried out by the fascist Iron Guard and the Croatian Ustase established a particularly notorious concentration camp at Jasenovac. In another at Loborgrad, 1500 Jewish women and girls were repeatedly raped by the camp guards. Camps were also established in Serbia, including at Zemun and Nis. Serbian fascists supported the Gestapo and the Wehrmacht in rounding up and killing Jews. Some Jews managed to escape to Italian occupation areas where anti-Semitic policies were only loosely enforced. In Salonika, the large Jewish community was first catalogued, then extorted and finally deported to the death camps. The Jewish community in Bulgaria itself, although not in the territories occupied by Bulgaria, fared somewhat better. Tsar Boris regarded the Jews as a bargaining chip and halted deportations when the war started to go against Germany.

## Albania

The Italians failed to win the hearts and minds of the Albanian people, adding arrogance to widespread corruption, which included the puppet government. Albanian attitudes shifted from indifference to hatred as the occupation wore on, reducing the number of collaborators, who were always stronger in the Catholic north of the country. Even the welcome expansion into Kosovo did little to kindle support for the Italians. Armed resistance started in early 1941, led primarily by the budding Communist Party and the puppet regime was unable to cope without the support of more than eight Italian divisions. When they left in 1943, the Germans reluctantly occupied Albania with no more than two and a half divisions stationed on the coast to protect against an Allied invasion threat.

The British were keen to take support for resistance groups further using Albania as a base. A Joint Planning Staff paper in May 1943 suggested landing four assault brigades and two infantry divisions at Durazzo, supported by air cover from the Italian mainland; a twentieth century version of the eleventh century Norman invasion of the Balkans. Churchill pursued the idea with General Alexander and Roosevelt, arguing that it would flare up the Balkans and force a German withdrawal to the Danube. However, the Americans were not for shifting and the scheme was buried at the Quadrant conference at Quebec.

Turkey maintained a strong interest in Albania through cultural and political ties (partly reflecting the Ottoman period until 1912), the significant Muslim population and opposition to Italy. In 1942, they even suggested to the Germans that Turkey could police Albania. The Turks supported King Zog as the only Muslim monarch in the Balkans and he was allowed to retain his legation in Istanbul amongst a significant émigré community. SOE also used Istanbul moneychangers to get funds into Albania.[25] The Turkish break with Germany in 1944 also damaged any hope the royalists had of using the German withdrawal to secure a non-communist government with international recognition.

## Greece

The Axis occupation of Greece was split between the three Axis invaders. The Bulgarians occupied western Thrace, the Germans the cities and Central Macedonia and the Italians the rest. After the Italian collapse, the Bulgarians took over Central Macedonia and the Germans the rest of the country.

Resistance in Greece began soon after the Axis occupation. There was a tradition of resistance in the mountains going back to Ottoman times and the Andartes viewed themselves as the reincarnation of that role. Greeks in urban areas also participated in small scale resistance activities, some organised by communists, setting the scene for later internal conflicts. From the end of 1942, British SOE liaison officers were parachuted into Greece as part of Churchill's plan to set Europe ablaze. Sabotage operations like blowing up the Gorgopotamos viaduct were successful but had a limited impact on German operations.

The Italian armistice was as confused in Greece as elsewhere. Most infamously, in the massacre of the Acqui Division on Cephalonia, the historical basis for the film *Captain Corelli's Mandolin*. Of 170,000 Italian troops in Greece, all but 40,000 surrendered, joined the resistance or just disappeared.[26] The competing resistance movements, ELAS and EDES, fought each other with the captured weapons. A Soviet military mission to ELAS made it clear that no help would be forthcoming. This reflected what became known as the Percentages Agreement between Churchill and Stalin, in which the Balkans were divided up into British and Soviet spheres of influence. Churchill claimed Greece while Stalin got Romania and Bulgaria. Tito went along with this, although he was also influenced by a falling out with the Bulgarian communists over Macedonia.[27]

The Turkish government supported King Zog throughout the war. Statue in Tirana. (MirkoS18, CC BY-SA 3.0)

The Corinth Canal was a vital waterway for the movement of Axis troops and supplies during the war. SOE made several attempts to block it. (Photo by Author)

Greece was to play an important role in the deception operation for Overlord during the summer of 1944 (Operation Zeppelin). Measures included prioritising military supplies and food to resistance groups in Crete and the Peloponnese to help convince the Germans that a landing was planned there. Actual Greek naval, land and air forces were moved into position west of Alexandria to reinforce this impression. Even famous Greek personalities were to be deployed, with associated publicity, to visit troops. However, Greek units were not deployed for real or dummy operations in Albania and Yugoslavia for political reasons. Interestingly, there was no similar objection to deploying the 1st Greek Division in the Ninth Army, which would have been deployed in Thrace.[28]

Despite the frosty diplomatic relationship in the spring of 1944, Turkey turned a blind eye to British naval units attacking German shipping in the Aegean from the Turkish coast, which included a supply base at Kusadasi, south of Izmir.

## Yugoslavia

The largest resistance forces in the Balkans were in Yugoslavia and by the end of 1941, there were two distinct groupings. The Chetniks, later recognised as the Yugoslav Army of the Homeland, commanded by Draza Mihailovic, was based in Central Serbia. They were predominately Serbian, royalist and anti-communist. This put them at odds with the partisans, later called the Yugoslav National Liberation Army, commanded by Josip 'Tito' Broz. The Axis forces controlled the main towns and lines of communication, which left the resistance groupings the mountains and countryside. There were seven major Axis offensives against the partisans, supported by collaborationist forces and sometimes by the Chetniks. This reflected the partisans willingness to attack the Axis, while the Chetniks were largely passive to avoid German reprisals.

The Italian armistice allowed Tito to equip his army, which had grown to around 200,000 men and women. Mihailovic never had quite the same degree of control of the varied groups of Chetniks, many of which tacitly and in some cases openly, collaborated with the Germans. The first priority of both factions was to destroy the other and place themselves in a position to control the post-war state. The Allies shifted their support to Tito at the end of 1943, when their analysis, supported by German intercepts, showed that the partisans were the only real resistance.[29] The British gave military considerations the priority in Yugoslavia, if not in Greece.

The Germans, especially Hitler, did believe an Allied landing was possible on the Dalmatian coast. In fact, there was a plan to establish a bridgehead on the Dalmatian coast called Operation Knockholt.[30] This impression was reinforced by the presence of regular British and some American forces on the island of Vis, commanded by Major-General Thomas Churchill (no relation).[31] This base included coastal forces and an airstrip, together with a partisan brigade. Raids took place against German garrisons and naval units on the islands and coastline.[32] Tito was briefly based there after the Germans nearly captured him at Drvar. The Allies also established the Balkan Air

The Allied airstrip on Vis is still visible today. (Photo by Author)

Tito's cave and command post on Vis. (Author)

Force to support partisan operations in Yugoslavia. This included nine RAF squadrons in ground attack and transport roles.

Turkey took a particular interest in their co-religionists in Bosnia. The Yugoslav Muslim Organisation (JMO) sought to keep their options open but Chetnik and Ustasha attacks pushed many Muslims towards the partisans. In late 1942, they asked the Germans for an autonomous area protected by the Wehrmacht. They also threatened to organise a mass emigration to Turkey and petitioned the Turkish National Assembly. Self-defence units expanded in several regions and Himmler used this as an opportunity to form the first SS division composed of non-Germans, the 13th Waffen SS Handschar Division.

## Romania

Romania joined the Axis in November 1940 and participated in the attack on the Soviet Union. It was an important supplier of oil and agricultural products to Germany. This made it a target for Allied bombing and was a significant factor in the drive to acquire airfields in Turkey. By August 1943, the oilfields around Ploesti could be reached from airfields in Italy and Libya. Operation Tidal Wave involved 178 B-24 Liberator bombers, of which only 88 returned.[33] The raid caused little damage to the oilfields and the Germans reinforced the anti-aircraft defences afterwards. A number of Liberators and 79 crew crash-landed in Turkey, where they were interned and the planes later deployed by the Turkish Air Force. They lived in the first-class Yeni Hotel in Ankara, lived pretty well on full pay and irritated the German ambassador at every opportunity. They were evacuated in stages, mainly through Syria, much to the relief of the Turkish authorities.

There was a small communist-led resistance movement in Romania. It engaged in the sabotage of war production but the impact was minimal after the security services arrested and executed all known communists. After the fall of Mussolini, some unofficial peace feelers came out from Hungary and Romania. Elements of the Romanian regime used the Turks as a conduit, By August 1944, the Red Army broke through the demoralised Romanian Army, braced with German units and advanced to the Carpathian-Danube line. This led to a palace coup that overthrew Ion Antonescu on 23 August and the King sued for peace. The British largely left it to the Soviets in accordance with the Percentages Agreement and delayed sending a mission.

## Bulgaria

Turkey's primary concern in early 1944 remained their border with Bulgaria, where the bulk of both armies faced each other. However, by the summer of 1944, it was clear to the Bulgarians that the Allies were likely to win the war. While Bulgaria had never declared war against the Soviet Union, few believed that would exempt the country from the Russian steamroller that was already attacking Romania to the north.

There was an active opposition within Bulgaria to the country joining the Axis and this turned into armed resistance after the invasion of the Soviet Union in 1941. In April 1943, the partisans were reorganised into the People's Liberation Rebel Army (NOVA). The war was brought directly to Bulgaria through the Allied bombing of Sofia, which caused significant damage to buildings and civilian casualties increased. Secret negotiations in March 1944 failed to persuade Bulgaria to switch sides when the Allies could not guarantee swift support.[34] The German response to the Italian capitulation demonstrated the risks. Part of the Allied offer was to use Greek and Turkish troops for the occupation, which was unacceptable to the Bulgarians and it is unclear how this would have been achieved.

A new government declared war on Germany but the Soviet Union had anticipated this move and declared war on Bulgaria on 5 September.

## Soviets Enter the Balkans

The Soviet 3rd Ukrainian Front switched from Romania into the Dobrudja region and reached the Bulgarian border on 6 September with four armies (46th, 37th, 57th, plus 4th Guards and 7th

USAAF 376th Bombardment Group over Sofia, Bulgaria, after an attack on the city. (United States Army Air Forces)

Mechanised Corps). Hitler believed the Soviets would go south into Turkey and take the Dardanelles, leaving a flanking force in Romania and Bulgaria.³⁵ The Soviets advanced without any preparatory artillery or air bombardment and quickly secured a crossing of the Danube. There was no resistance and the armoured spearhead quickly advanced, covering nearly 70km on the first day, usually greeted joyfully by the population. The port of Varna fell on 8 September, supported by the Soviet Black Sea fleet and the 83rd Marine Infantry Brigade. Burgas fell to a similar operation without resistance from the Bulgarian Navy, while the Germans scuttled their naval units.

One Soviet Army was transferred back to Romania while mechanised and air units swung round towards Sofia, entering the city on 15 September. Instead of immediately regrouping and moving westwards to cut off the retreating Germans, Stavka ordered a concentration of forces in eastern Bulgaria, supported by additional air and naval units for around 20 days. The command of the 4th Guards Mechanised Corps planned two operations, one south and another to the west. This unit alone had 157 T-34 tanks and 42 SU-85 self-propelled guns, which would have presented a major problem for the Turkish armoured brigades. Like Hitler, the German Army Group Commander (Heeresgruppe F) von Weichs believed they were positioned for an attack on Turkey because there were no German units to attack in that direction.

It remains unclear if Stalin was planning an offensive against Turkey, or at least suggesting to the Western Allies and Turkey that he might. The Soviet 37th Army with the Black Sea Fleet and 17th Air Army remained at full combat readiness for an attack on Turkey up to 13 October. Tito, Dimitrov and Stalin met in Moscow on 25–27 September to agree on the entry of Soviet and Bulgarian armies into Yugoslavia. The focus was the capture of Belgrade, which fell on 19 October. However, stiff German resistance meant that (Heeresgruppe F) von Weichs and E (Lohr) managed to retreat to new defensive lines in northern Yugoslavia.

The new Greek government reached Athens on 18 October. Sadly, for Greece, national political unity did not last for long and by December, civil war had broken out. Stalin stuck to the Percentages Agreement and no Soviet troops entered Greece.

The British fleet in the Aegean was strengthened by releasing carriers from the invasion of southern France (Operation Dragoon). Seven carriers, with cruisers and destroyers, took part in Operation Outing, which aimed to support British landings on the islands and harass the German withdrawal. German naval units were sunk and their communications severed. This was followed by air attacks on airfields and land bases in five distinct phases. A few damaged aircraft made forced landings in Turkey, including a Hellcat from HMS *Emperor*, damaged during an attack on Crete and was diverted

Russian T34 tanks would have been a major threat to the Turkish armoured brigades in Thrace. (Photo by Author, Belgrade Kalemegdan)

to Gokova in Turkey rather than make an attempt to land on the carrier. The pilot returned to his ship a few weeks later and took part in the final phase of Operation Outing.³⁶ Clearly, at this stage in the war, internment was not too onerous.

The Red Army did not enter Albania and communist forces took power as the Germans retreated. Much fighting went on in the western Balkans and in Hungary. The last German units in the Balkans were not disarmed until May 1945.

The Soviet domination of the Balkans encouraged the new Greek government to consider a Greek-Turkish alliance. Although Turkey's avoidance of military occupation, abandoning Greece in 1940–1941 and the discrimination against Greeks through the *Varlik* wealth tax, all rankled with the Greeks. The British, particularly Eden, encouraged this, although it remained anxious not to give the impression it was assuming a post-war rivalry with the Soviet Union. This was reflected in the decision on 16 September not to supply additional military equipment to Turkey, which could only be interpreted as an anti-Soviet measure given that there was no longer a window for Turkish military action against Germany.

**Turkey Declares War**

Turkey was in an ambiguous position as the Soviets rolled into the Balkans because it was not covered by the Percentages Agreement. Although the Turks did not know this at the time, Stalin had also served notice on Churchill at their October 1944 meeting in Moscow, that he would be seeking revisions to the Montreux Convention on the Straits. Eden viewed a new Anglo-Turkish alliance as the cornerstone of British policy in the eastern Mediterranean. However, he appears not to have communicated that position to Churchill before the October 1944 Moscow conference at which Churchill only referenced the Montreux Convention.³⁷

While Turkey had broken off diplomatic relations with Germany, it had not declared war. As ever, Turkey was more concerned about the Soviets than they had ever been about Germany. The establishment of a communist government in Bulgaria was another concern because it could raise long-standing territorial issues backed by the Soviet Union. A problem magnified by speeches made by the new Bulgarian government and pan-Slavic statements by Tito. Turkey welcomed British intervention in Greece and played their part by declaring they had no claim on the Dodecanese islands.

With the Soviet 37th Army on the border, the Turkish army reorganised, putting their best equipment into the west, using the old R35 and T26 tanks in airfield defence or in fixed fortifications. The First Army included the 3rd Armoured Division, which had nearly 180 medium and 90 light tanks. However, most of these tanks were obsolete compared to the battle-hardened Soviet veterans facing them with T34 tanks. The arrival of 104 Spitfire Vs in the autumn of 1944 significantly improved Turkish air cover, together with an effective offensive capacity using Baltimore bombers and Beaufighter Xs for anti-shipping operations.

One of the first acts of the new Turkish Foreign Minister, Hasan Saka, was to break off diplomatic relations with Japan, following a request by the US Ambassador. More significantly, they allowed war material for the Soviet Union to travel through the Straits.

At the Yalta conference in February 1945, the Big Three nations agreed on a range of proposals on the post-war order, which included a somewhat vacuous Declaration on Liberated Europe that created few problems for Stalin. More importantly for Turkey, it was agreed that only those nations that had declared war on Germany should be granted the status of an Associated Nation of the United Nations. Stalin had used Turkey as an example to illustrate his proposal and attacked their wavering whilst they speculated on who would be on the winning side. Churchill defended Turkey and pressed the benefits of a declaration of war on German morale. On this basis, a deadline was set for the end of February. Churchill also accepted that the Montreux Convention should be revised, including free Soviet passage, subject to respecting the independence and integrity of Turkey.

In this context, Turkey moved quickly to a declaration of war. It was dressed up to the National Assembly as a natural consequence of Turkey's alliance with Britain and friendship with the Soviet Union. However, the reality was that Turkey was in no position to refuse and it could also do so, at no military risk. This was a point strongly made by the Soviets, who in March ended the Turko-Soviet Treaty of Neutrality and Non-aggression, which had been agreed in 1925 and extended several times. The Turks sought a new treaty and attempted to put a positive spin on the developments but the Soviets were in no rush and the Russian media stepped up its attacks. Turkey's late declaration of war gave it limited influence at the San Francisco conference, which finalised the Charter of the United Nations. Britain supported Turkey's interests in the Balkans but the Balkan states, particularly Yugoslavia, disagreed. Turkey also opposed the veto powers of the Big Five nations in the Charter but recognised the political realities.

While the Turks remained concerned about the Soviets in Bulgaria, they offered to provide a couple of divisions to fight in Italy. However, General Alexander was sceptical that Turkish forces were in any shape to participate without burdening Allied resources.[38] He conceded that they could be useful if they arrived by the end of May and recommended sending a military mission to Ankara. The end of the war in Europe meant that nothing came of this initiative.

The war finishing did not end the tensions between Turkey and the Soviet Union. In June, the Soviets demanded the cession of Kars and Ardahan in eastern Turkey and Soviet military and legal control of the Straits regime. Turkey was also concerned over Soviet support for the Armenians and an independent Kurdistan, although Soviet sources imply this was used more as a bargaining chip. Despite the cooling of relations in 1944, the British defended Turkish interests strongly, supporting access but not bases in the Straits. The Soviets made obvious comparisons with the Panama and Suez canals and Gibraltar, a point the incoming British Prime Minister, Clement Atlee, had some sympathy with.

The Americans decided to hold back initially but the adoption of the Truman Doctrine put Greece and Turkey on the front line of the new Cold War and Turkey became an important US ally. While Stalin looked to pursue Soviet interests in Turkey and their southern periphery more generally, his priority was central and Eastern Europe, which meant restraint in any conflict in the region.[39] He also now had bases in Bulgaria with which he could threaten the Straits.

# 9
# CONCLUSION

The nineteenth century 'great man' view of history is less fashionable today, even when de-gendered into the 'big beast' theory. However, in our story, it is hard not to focus on two key players – Churchill and İnönü. Both men played a decisive role in driving the policies of their respective countries.

Winston Churchill was the Prime Minister in a democracy but he had an extraordinary influence on the direction of the war, both in Britain and arguably amongst the Allied powers. It was Churchill who almost alone pursued the 'soft underbelly' strategy, which included efforts to get Turkey into the Second World War. Churchill's optimism regarding Turkey is difficult to understand, given both the advice he was given by diplomats and military advisers as well as the intelligence decrypts. The Foreign Office's Southern Department, which also had access to the diplomatic decrypts, consistently believed that Turkey would not enter the war.

Later, during the war, Churchill's concern over Soviet expansion also drove this Turkish strategy. Alan Brooke confided to his diaries his frustrations with Churchill's scattergun approach to strategy,[1] supporting one operation after another and more often wanting them all simultaneously. Planning staff wasted many days addressing the outputs from his fertile mind as the long list of operations never carried out, shows.[2] Brooke recorded that 'Winston had ten ideas a day, only one of which is good and he did not know which one it was'.

Soviet policy was at best inconsistent, latterly turning firmly against Turkish entry into the war as it might interfere with their post-war plans for the Balkans. They used Turkish trade with Germany and pan-Turanism as examples of Turkish wartime collaboration to press their claims in eastern Turkey and the Straits. The Americans reluctantly played along with Churchill so long as it did not detract from the invasion of France, allowing the British to take the lead on Turkey. Even Churchill's military and political colleagues were lukewarm about Turkey. Churchill was aided by Hitler's interest in the Balkans, driven primarily by economic factors. This was backed up by the resilience of the German military in the region, which achieved much with limited resources.

İnönü was the President of the Turkish Republic, which at best was only a partial democracy. He directed foreign policy and made all the major judgement calls with, as far as we can tell, little internal opposition to his policy of noninterventionism. We also know from the diplomatic decrypts that Turkish officials all worked on the basis that Turkey would not become a belligerent unless the country was attacked. It could reasonably be argued that Turkish neutrality in 1940 avoided the French and British from engaging in any one of the proposed Balkans and Caucasus schemes, which could have resulted in a two-front war with Germany and the Soviet Union. The state of Turkish armed forces in 1940 would, in any case, have made Turkey more of a liability than an Allied asset. It could also have opened up the Middle East to Germany without the trials of the Western Desert campaign.

As one of the warrior diplomats, İnönü recognised the risks of war and the need to allow Turkey to rebuild its economy after the wars of the early years of the century. Most scholars present İnönü's presidency as continuity with that of Atatürk. While his programme was an extension of his predecessor's domestic and foreign policies, he also had to adapt them to address the new internal and external challenges that arose in the Second World War. He understood that the Turkish armed forces were not prepared for war, even with military equipment provided by the Allies. The published memoirs of Turkish officers confirm the pessimistic reports of Allied and Axis officers in Turkey.

Turkey was not neutral in the strictest sense; it was non-belligerent. It never renounced its Treaty with Britain and France, even if it avoided its more active provisions. President İnönü openly stated that he expected the Allies to win the war, which undoubtedly influenced his position. The British Ambassador summed this up well in 1942 as, '… sitting on the fence but at least they are sitting with their faces in our direction and their backs to Germany, though continually squinting over their shoulders to see what danger is brewing behind them – and always squinting sideways at Russia'.[3]

Apart from a brief period when Germany did seriously consider invading Turkey (Operation Gertrud), Hitler's position towards Turkey was straightforward. Stay neutral and that includes not allowing any use of Turkish territory to attack the Axis. If you do not, we will retaliate by bombing Istanbul. No offer from the British of anti-aircraft guns or even RAF squadrons would convince the Turks that they could defend against this threat. While the Germans probably could have invaded Turkey in 1942, it would have required a commitment of up to 20 divisions, many of which would have to remain for garrison duties along their lines of communications.

If access to the Middle East was the aim, or even the grandiose link up with the Japanese (Operation Orient), many in Germany thought this could be achieved via the Caucasus. We should also remember that Turkey and the eastern Mediterranean were never Hitler's main focus. His military made a good case for a peripheral strategy to knock out Britain from the Middle East in 1940, which included attacking Turkey. However, Hitler was operating in a broader context and the entry of the Soviet Union and America into the conflict was the deciding factor of the war.

The war also directly impacted Turkey and its economy, with more than a million men in the armed forces by 1942 out of a total population of 17.8 million. In contrast, 650,000 worked in industry. Military expenditure increased from 94 million TL in 1938 to 554 million TL in 1944, more than half the total government budget. Real wages dropped by 40 percent and bread rations were cut by half in May 1942. Without trade unions, which were banned, workers fled dangerous industries and villages for the towns. War profiteering added to the criticism and a common protest was to burn the ears off İnönü's portrait on banknotes. İnönü was given credit for keeping Turkey out of the war but he was viewed as less successful in addressing domestic issues. One story illustrates his position. When visiting a village, he faced a mother who angrily criticised him because she had to pay five *liras* for her daughter's milk. His reply was: 'But I haven't made her fatherless'.

Turkey's prime consideration as the war progressed was the Soviet Union, something that the British underestimated throughout the war. Turkey did not want the Soviets in the Balkans at any price and consistently referenced the absence of Soviet guarantees when pressed by the British to join the war. So much so that they may have unintentionally thwarted British efforts to get the Axis satellite states in the Balkans to surrender before the Red Army arrived. This made Soviet domination of the region inevitable, which almost resulted in Stalin attacking Turkey itself in October 1944. Churchill has been criticised for the Percentages Agreement but in practice, he simply recognised the strength of the Soviet position in the Balkans.

The success of any 'soft underbelly' strategy was always doubtful, quite apart from the American resistance to the numerous plans promoted by Churchill and his military planners. The plans set out broad strategic objectives but did not address the practical challenges of getting large amounts of men and materials through the Balkans to Vienna. It would have required a complete collapse of the German military. Something which happened in 1918 but in 1944–1945, as Kesselring's defence of Italy showed, the German army was more resilient. It took the Soviet steamroller, with many more divisions than the western Allies could even dream of putting into the Balkans to get the job done. If it was not for the Americans insisting on Overlord, Churchill might have frittered away scarce resources on operations that had limited potential.

That does not mean action in the Mediterranean had no impact on the war. The many strategic deception operations involving Turkey and the Balkan states successfully held German troops in the region that could have been deployed more effectively elsewhere. The modest investment in men and materials paid dividends in terms of defeating Hitler.

Britain's efforts to push Turkey into the war failed, although it did at least keep Turkey out of the Axis camp, which would have had serious military consequences in 1939–1941. The diplomatic strategy had worked in a divided Yugoslavia in 1941 but failed against a united Turkey. While the consequences of support for resistance groups have been criticised, most would have happened anyway and Allied support was not decisive. There was little Britain could have done to restrain the Soviet domination of the Balkans. In any case, British military priorities were the defeat of Germany, in which post-war political considerations took second place. Had Germany not invaded the Soviet Union in 1941 and instead swept south into the Mediterranean, it is doubtful whether Britain would have been on the winning side in Europe, even with later US support. Victory in Europe was dependent on the Red Army.

# APPENDICES

## I

## MAIN CHARACTERS

**Brooke, Alan**
As the CIGS for most of the war, Alan Brooke was Churchill's primary military adviser. A career soldier, he came from a noble military family in Ulster. He served in the artillery during WW1 and commanded II Corps during the Battle for France.

He took over as CIGS in December 1941 and became chairman of the Chiefs of Staff Committee in March 1942. He was publicly supportive of Churchill's Mediterranean strategy, which regularly brought him into conflict with the Americans. However, as his diaries show, while he admired Churchill's leadership, he was frustrated by Churchill's inconsistent meddling in military strategy. He died in 1963.

**Çakmak, Fevzi**
The Chief of the General Staff of the Turkish army was born in Istanbul in 1876. His father was an artillery colonel and he went through a military education, including the War College and Staff Academy, graduating in 1898. He served in the Balkans, including in the Vardar Army during the Balkan Wars. In the First World War, he served in the Gallipoli campaign as the commander of V Corps before commanding the Second Army on the Caucasus front and then the Seventh Army in Syria. In 1918 he was appointed Chief of the General Staff and then Minister of War in the Ottoman Government.

Despite his initial doubts, he joined the nationalists in 1920 and became Minister of National Defence, commanding with Kemal at the critical battles of Sakarya and Dumlupinar. He subsequently became Prime Minister until July 1922, when he was appointed Chief of the General Staff until his retirement in 1944. He entered politics in 1946 and helped found the Nation Party in 1948. He died in Istanbul in 1950.

**Churchill, Winston**
The Prime Minister of the United Kingdom during the Second World War was born in 1874. In his early military career, he saw action in India, Sudan and South Africa before entering politics. In the First World War, as First Lord of the Admiralty, he presided over the disastrous Gallipoli campaign, which he hoped would knock the Ottoman Empire out of the war. Along with his strong imperialist views, he retained an interest in Turkey, visiting the country several times and was an admirer of Atatürk, writing a glowing tribute on his death.

He opposed Chamberlain's appeasement policy and became Prime Minister in 1940. During the war, Churchill doggedly pursued a policy of bringing Turkey into the conflict as part of his Mediterranean strategy for Germany's defeat. He even visited Turkey during the war to personally appeal to İnönü. Despite his frustration over the Turkish government's response, he supported Turkey against Stalin's territorial claims at the end of the war. Churchill lost the 1945 election but returned to power in 1951, still focused on protecting the British Empire and strengthening British-American relations in the face of the Cold War. This included bringing Turkey and Greece into NATO. He died in 1965.

**İnönü, Ismet**
The President of the Republic of Turkey throughout the Second World War was born in Izmir in 1884. From a military family, he had a military education in the artillery before graduating from the Staff Academy in 1906. During the Yemen revolt (1910–1913), he was the Chief of Staff and served in the Çatalca Army HQ during the Balkan Wars. In the First World War, he served with Kemal on the Caucasian and Palestine fronts before moving to the posts in the Ministry of war.

He joined the nationalists in 1920 and commanded the northern section of the Western Front, winning the battles of İnönü from which his surname was taken in 1934. He was the chief delegate and signatory of the Lausanne peace treaty in July 1923 before being appointed Prime Minister and Minister of Foreign Affairs. He was Prime Minister on four separate occasions, finally relinquishing the post in 1937 after disagreements over the economy with Atatürk.

He was elected President on the death of Atatürk (with the title 'National Chief') in 1938 and served three terms until his party was defeated in the 1950 elections. He kept Turkey out of the Second World War until February 1945, although his domestic policies were much less popular and contributed to his post-war defeat. He remained in politics until his death in 1973 at the age of 89.

**Knatchbull-Hugessen, Hughe**
He was the British ambassador to Turkey during the Second World War. A career diplomat, he was almost killed by a Japanese fighter aircraft near Shanghai in 1937. As ambassador to Turkey from 1939, he was the main channel for the British policy of pressurising Turkey to join the Allies. He is probably best known for the Cicero spy scandal when his poor security allowed his valet to steal important papers and sell them to the Germans. After the war, he was ambassador to Belgium and then Luxembourg before retiring in 1947.

**Menemencioğlu, Numan**
This career diplomat was Turkey's Minister of Foreign Affairs for much of the Second World War. He was born in Pirlepe in 1880 into a political family and joined the foreign service after university. He served in various ambassadorial roles across Europe and Beirut before returning to the Ministry in Ankara in 1928. His next appointment was secretary-general of the Ministry of Foreign Affairs in 1937 and became foreign minister in August 1942. He was dismissed in June 1944 after pressure from Churchill due to his perceived pro-German views and served as the ambassador to Paris from 1944 until retirement in 1956. He then re-entered politics but died in Ankara in 1958.

### von Papen, Franz

The former Chancellor of Germany was the German ambassador to Turkey during the Second World War. He was trained as a staff officer and served on the Western Front and with the Ottoman Army in the Middle East during the First World War. After the war, he entered politics and enabled Hitler's rise to power, believing he could keep him in check. He was then appointed ambassador to Turkey until diplomatic relations were ended in 1944. As ambassador, he failed to halt the alliance with Britain and France but built stronger links after the defeat of France in 1940. He secured important economic contracts and the supply of raw materials, followed by a treaty of friendship in June 1941. His influence waned along with Germany's retreat from Russia and he resorted to threats of bombardment if Turkey joined the Allies. He left Turkey and retired when diplomatic relations were terminated in 1944. He was acquitted of war crimes at Nuremberg but sentenced to hard labour by a West German denazification court. He died in 1969.

### Saracoğlu, Şükrü

The Foreign Minister and Prime Minister of Turkey for much of the Second World War was born in Ödemis in 1887. He studied in Istanbul and Geneva before becoming a civil servant and a teacher. He was elected to the Grand National Assembly in 1923 and held various ministerial posts, including education, finance and justice, before becoming Minister of Foreign affairs in 1938. He was appointed Prime Minister in July 1942 and served until his retirement due to ill health in 1946. He died in 1953 in Istanbul.

### Wilson, Henry Maitland

Known as Jumbo Wilson, he commanded British forces in the eastern Mediterranean during most of the Second World War. A career soldier, he served in the Boer War, Egypt, India and on the Western Front in the First World War. In 1939 he was appointed as GOC Egypt, then the expeditionary force to Greece in 1941, followed by the 9th Army in Syria, GOC Middle East and finally, Supreme Allied Commander in the Mediterranean from January 1944. He was the key military adviser on efforts to get Turkey to join the war and a supporter of Churchill's indirect strategy. He died in 1964.

# II
# CHRONOLOGY

|  |  |
| --- | --- |
| July 1923 | Treaty of Lausanne. Established the post First World War borders of Turkey |
| October 1923 | Proclamation of the Republic of Turkey with Mustafa Kemal as President |
| December 1925 | Non-aggression treaty with the Soviet Union (renewed 1935) |
| October 1927 | Mustafa Kemal's 'Nutuk' speech, which set out the principles of Kemalism |
| October 1930 | Ankara Treaty of friendship and peace with Greece |
| July 1932 | Turkey joins the League of Nations |
| February 1934 | Balkan Pact between Turkey, Greece, Romania and Yugoslavia |
| July 1936 | Montreux Convention on the future regime for the Straits |
| July 1937 | Saadabad Pact between Turkey, Iraq, Iran and Afghanistan |
| November 1938 | Death of Atatürk and succession of İnönü as President of Turkey |
| April 1939 | Italy occupies Albania |
| May/June 1939 | Treaties between Britain, France and Turkey. Hatay transferred to Turkey |
| August 1939 | Russia and Germany sign a non-aggression pact |
| Summer 1939 | Turkish army manoeuvres in Thrace highlighted military deficiencies |
| September 1939 | Germany invades Poland at the start of the Second World War |
| October 1939 | Ankara conference on Turkish military requirements in the event of war |
| January 1940 | National Protection (Defence) Law put Turkey on a war footing |
| February 1940 | Final meeting of Balkan Pact fails to reach agreement on military action |
| June 1940 | Turkey refuses the Allied request to join the war |
| October 1940 | Italy invades Greece |
| April 1941 | Iraq coup. It collapsed by May after the British invasion |
| February 1941 | Turkish-Bulgarian treaty of friendship |
| February 1941 | Operation Abstention, British capture and later withdrawal from the island of Kastelorizo off the Turkish coast |
| March 1941 | Bulgaria joins the Axis |
| March 1941 | Germany invades Yugoslavia and Greece (Operation Marita) |
| June 1941 | Turkey and Germany sign non-aggression treaty |
| June 1941 | Germany invades the Soviet Union |
| June 1941 | British invasion of Syria against Vichy France |
| August 1941 | British and Soviet invasion of Iran |
| October 1941 | Clodius Agreement. Turkish supply of chromite to Germany |
| December 1941 | Japan attacks the USA and Germany and Italy declare war on the USA |
| September 1942 | German military loans to Turkey, followed by equipment supplies |
| November 1942 | Wealth tax introduced in Turkey that mostly impacted non-Muslims |
| December 1942 | Planned date for Operation Gertrud. The German invasion of Turkey (abandoned 1943) |
| January 1943 | Casablanca conference. Allies seek Turkish entry to the war |
| January 1943 | Adana meeting: Churchill travels to Turkey to press entry to the war |

| | | | |
|---|---|---|---|
| Summer 1943 | Operation Hardihood. Allied equipment and training for Turkey | January 1944 | Turkish Air Force Command established as a separate branch |
| July 1943 | Fall of Mussolini. Italy leaves the Axis | February 1944 | Turkey refuses to meet the Allied deadline. Allied relations deteriorate |
| September 1943 | Failed British attempt to capture islands in the Dodecanese (Accolade) | March 1944 | Start of Operation Zeppelin deception operations in the eastern Mediterranean |
| October 1943 | Moscow conference. Soviets call for Turkey to end neutrality | April 1944 | Turkey stops chromite exports to Germany and hardens diplomatic relations |
| October 1943–April 1944 | Operation Cicero. German intelligence steal documents from the British embassy in Ankara | August 1944 | Turkey breaks off diplomatic relations with Germany |
| November 1943 | Tehran conference confirmed Turkey should enter war in 1944 | September 1944 | Red Army reaches Bulgarian border |
| | | February 1945 | Turkey declares war on Germany |
| December 1943 | Cairo conference addressed details of Turkey's entry into the war | May 1945 | Last German units in the Balkans disarmed. Germany surrenders |

# BIBLIOGRAPHY

Anon, *Turkish Officers – WWII memories* (Ankara: General Staff Military History and Strategic Studies Department, 1999)

Alexiades, P., *Target Corinth Canal 1940–44* (Yorkshire: Pen & Sword, 2015)

Appleby, S., *SYMBOL: Churchill, Roosevelt and the Casablanca Conference* (London: Bookswarm, 1998)

Avci, A., *Winning the war of perception: American attempts to counter Germany's military influence in Turkey during World War II* (Turkish Studies, Nov. 2015)

Bailey, R., *The Wildest Province* (London: Jonathan Cape, 2008)

Balfour, N., *Paul of Yugoslavia – Britain's Maligned Friend* (London: Hamish Hamilton, 1980)

Barber, L., *Freyberg: Churchill's Salamander* (London: Hutchinson, 1990)

Barker, E., *British Policy in South-East Europe in the Second World War* (London: MacMillan, 1976)

Barker, E., Chadwick, J, Deakin, W, *British Political and Military Strategy in Central, Eastern and Southern Europe in 1944* (London: Palgrave Macmillan, 1988)

Barlas, D., *Friends or Foes? Diplomatic Relations between Italy and Turkey, 1923–36 International Journal of Middle East Studies*, Vol.36, No.2, May 2004

Barno, D., & Bensahel, N, *Adaptation Under Fire: How Militaries Change in Wartime* (Oxford, 2020)

Barr, J., *A Line in the Sand* (London, Simon and Shuster, 2011)

Belot, R., *The Struggle for the Mediterranean 1939–45* (Princeton, 1951)

Benyon-Tinker, W., *Dust upon the Sea* (London: Hodder & Stoughton, 1947)

Bezci, E., 'Turkey's intelligence diplomacy during the Second World War', *Journal of Intelligence History*, 15:2, pp.80–95

Blau, G., *Invasion Balkans!: The German Campaign in the Balkans, Spring 1941* (Shippensburg, PA, Burd Street, 1997)

Brewer, D., *Greece, The Decade of War* (London: I.B.Tauris, 2016)

Bulloch, J., *No Friends but the Mountains* (New York: Viking, 1992)

Carr, J., *The Defence and Fall of Greece 1940–41* (Yorkshire: Pen & Sword, 2013)

Catherwood, C, *The Balkans in World War Two: Britain's Balkan Dilemma* (London: Palgrave, 2003)

Catherwood, C., *Churchill and Tito* (Yorkshire: Front-line, 2017)

Cervi, M., *The Hollow Legions: Mussolini's Blunder in Greece* (New York: Doubleday, 1971)

Churchill, W., *The Second World War Vol.5 Closing the Ring* (New York: Rosetta Books, 2013)

Ciano, G., Edited by Muggeridge, M, *Ciano's Diary 1939–1943* (Portsmouth: New Hampshire, Heinemann, 1947)

Corse, E., 'To accustom Turkish minds to a state of belligerency': *The Delicate Balance of British Propaganda in Turkey during the Second World War* (Journal of Balkan and Near Eastern Studies, Sept 2021)

Cox, G., *The Race for Trieste* (London: William Kimber, 1977)

Creveld, M., *Hitler's Strategy 1940–41 – The Balkan Clue* (Cambridge, 1973)

Cruickshank, C., *Deception in World War 2* (London: Book Club Associates, 1979)

Danchev, A. and Todman, D., *War Diaries of Field Marshall Lord Alanbrooke* (London: W&N, 2001)

Davidson, B., *Special Operations Europe* (London: Victor Gollancz, 1980)

Deakin, F.W.D., *The Embattled Mountain* (Oxford, 1971)

Denniston, R., *Churchill's Secret War: Diplomatic Decrypts, the Foreign Office and Turkey 1942–44* (Stroud, Gloucestershire: History Press, 2009)

Djilas, M., *Wartime* (New York: Harcourt Brace Jovanovich, 1977)

Denniston, R., *Churchill's Secret War: Diplomatic Decrypts, the Foreign Office and Turkey, 1942–44* (Stroud, Gloucestershire: Sutton, 1997)

Deringil, S., *Turkish Foreign Policy During the Second World War* (Cambridge, 1989)

*Documents on German Foreign Policy 1918–1945* (HMSO, 1957–83)

Dollmann, E., *With Hitler and Mussolini – Memoirs of a Nazi Interpreter* (New York: Skyhorse, 2017)

Dugan,J., *Ploesti* (New York: Random House, 1982)

Ehrman, J., *Grand Strategy: Volume V* (HMSO, 1956)

Elliott, N., *Never Judge a Man by his Umbrella* (London, 1991)

Erikson, Edward, *The Turkish War of Independence* (Westport, Connecticut: Praeger, 2021)

Fischer, B., *Albania at War 1939–1945* (West Lafayette, Indiana: Purdue, 1999)

Fort, A., *Wavell: Life and Times of an Imperial Servant* (London: Jonathan Cape, 2011)
Forczyk, R., *The Caucasus 1942–43: Kleist's Race for Oil* (Oxford: Osprey, 2015)
Freeman, G., *The Forgotten 500* (New York: NAL, 2007)
Gartzonikas, P., *Amphibious and Special Operations in the Aegean Sea 1943–45* (Naval Postgraduate School Thesis, California, 2003)
Gerolymatos, A., *The Balkan Wars* (Yorkshire: Spellmount, 2004)
Glantz, D., *Red Storm over the Balkans* (Kansas, 2007)
Glenny, M., *The Balkans 1804–1999* (London: Granta Books, 1999)
Gökçen, S., *A Life Along the Path of Atatürk* (Ankara: Turkish Aviation League, 1981)
Gorodetsky, G., *Grand Delusion: Stalin and the German Invasion of Russia* (New Haven, 1999)
Gorenberg, G., *War of Shadows: Codebreakers, Spies and the Secret Struggle to Drive the Nazis from the Middle East* (Public Affairs, 2021)
Gould, A., *Special Duties: Reminiscences of a RAF staff officer in the Balkans, Turkey and the Middle East* (London: Sampson Low, Marston & Co, 1945)
Guard, J., *Improvise and Dare* (London: Book Guild, 1997)
Gurboga, N., *Mine Workers, The State and War* (Istanbul: Bogazici University, 2005)
Guvenc, S., *Building a Republican Navy in Turkey: 1924–1939*, International Journal of Naval History, Vol.1 No.1, April 2002
Hakki, M., 'Surviving the Pressure of the Superpowers: An Analysis of Turkish Neutrality During the Second World War', *Journal of Military and Strategic Studies*, 2006, Vol.8, Issue 2.
Hamilton, N., *Monty, Master of the Battlefield 1942–44* (London, Hamish Hamilton, 1983)
Hammond, R., *Strangling the Axis: The Fight for Control of the Mediterranean during the Second World War* (Cambridge UP, 2020)
Heper, M., *The State and Kurds in Turkey* (London, Palgrave, 2007)
Holt, Thaddeus, *The Deceivers: Allied Military Deception in the Second World War* (New York: Lisa Drew Books, 2004)
Hobbs, D., *Taranto and Naval warfare in the Mediterranean 1940–1945* (Yorkshire: Seaforth, 2020)
Hoptner, J., *Yugoslavia in Crisis 1934–41* (Columbia, 1963)
Howard, M., *The Mediterranean Strategy in the Second World War* (Barnsley, Yorkshire: Greenhill, 1993)
Howard, M., *Grand Strategy: Volume IV* (HMSO, Kindle edition, 2016)
Howard, M., *British Intelligence in the Second World War, Vol.5* (HMSO, 1990)
Irving, D., *The Trail of the Fox* (London: BCA edition, 1977)
Isci, O., *Turkey and the Soviet Union During World War II* (London: I.B.Tauris, 2019)
Isci, O., (2020). 'The Massigli Affair and its Context: Turkish Foreign Policy after the Molotov–Ribbentrop Pact', *Journal of Contemporary History*, 55(2), pp.271–296)
James, B., *Hitler's Gulf War* (Yorkshire: Pen & Sword, 2009)
Jennings, C., *Flashpoint Trieste* (Oxford: Osprey, 2017)
Jowett, P., *Armies of the Greek-Turkish War 1919-22* (Oxford: Osprey, 2015)
Kepher, Stephen, *Cossac: Lt.Gen. Sir Frederick Morgan and the Genesis of Operation Overlord* (Annapolis: Naval Institute Press, 2020)
King, C., *Midnight at the Pera Palace* (New York & London: Norton, 2015)
Kinross, P., *Atatürk: The Rebirth of a Nation* (London: W&N, 2001)
Kousoulas, D., *The Price of Freedom: Greece in World Affairs 1939–53* (Aukland: Pickle, 2016)
Leiser, G., 'The Turkish Air Force 1939–45', *Middle Eastern Studies*, Vol.26, No.3, pp.383–395
Lepre, G., *Himmler's Bosnian Division* (Atglen, PA: Schiffer, 1997)
Leverkuehn, P., *German Military Intelligence* (Kindle edition: Lucknow Books, 2016)
Lindsay, F., *Beacons in the Night* (Stanford, 1993)
Lihou, M., *Out of the Italian Night* (Shrewsbury, England: Airlife, 2003)
Lintott, B., *The Mediterranean Double-Cross System, 1941–1945* (Abington, England: Routledge, 2018)
Livanios, D., *The Macedonian Question Britain and the Southern Balkans 1939–1949* (Oxford, 2008)
Lulushi, A., *Donovan's Devils* (New York: Arcade, 2016)
Macintyre, B., *Operation Mincemeat* (London: Bloomsbury, 2010)
Maclean, F., *Eastern Approaches* (London: Jonathan Cape, 1949)
Matev, K., *The Armoured Forces of the Bulgarian Army 1936-45* (Warwick: Helion, 2015)
Matev, K., *Red Wind Over the Balkans* (Warwick: Helion, 2019)
May, E., *Strange Victory: Hitler's Conquest of France* (New York: Hill and Wang, 2015)
McConville, M., *A Small War in the Balkans* (London: MacMillan, 1986)
McDowall, D., *A Modern History of the Kurds* (London: I.B.Tauris, 2004)
McHugo, J., *Syria: A Recent History* (London:Saqi, 2015)
McMeekin, S., *The Berlin-Baghdad Express* (London: Allan Lane, 2010)
McMeekin, S., *Stalin's War* (London: Penguin, 2021)
Millman, B., *The Ill-Made Alliance: Anglo-Turkish Relations 1934–1940* (McGill-Queens University Press, 1998)
Milton, N., *Neville Chamberlain's Legacy* (Yorkshire: Pen and Sword, 2019)
Mladenov, A., *The Bulgarian Air Force in the Second World War* (Warwick: Helion, 2018)
Moyzisch, L., *Operation Cicero* (Wingate, 1950)
Nicolson, N., *Alex* (London: Weidenfeld & Nicolson, 1973)
Napier, S., *Churchill Military Genius or Menace?* (Stroud, Gloucestershire: History Press, 2018)
Nikolajsen, O., *Turkish Military Aircraft Since 1912* (Ankara: Ucanturk aviation magazine)
Nikoloudis, N., *The Sacred Squadron*, (PhD dissertation, Kings College London)
Nur Altinors, M., *Turkish Foreign policy during WW2* (Asian Journal of Social Science Studies, Vol. 2, No. 4, 2017)
Oakley-Hill, D., *An Englishman in Albania* (London: Centre for Albanian Studies, 2002)
O'Carroll, B., *The Long Range Desert Group in the Aegean* (Yorkshire: Pen & Sword, 2020)
Office of the Historian, Bureau of Public Affairs, United States Department of State. *The Conferences at Washington, 1941–1942 and Casablanca, 1943* (Foreign Relations of the United States)
*The Conferences at Cairo and Tehran, 1943* (Foreign Relations of the United States: Diplomatic Papers, 1943)
O'Hara, V., *Struggle for the Middle Sea* (Annapolis: Naval Institute Press, 2009)
O'Sullivan, A., *Nazi Secret Warfare in Occupied Persia (Iran)* (London: Palgrave, 2014)

O'Sullivan, A., *Espionage and Counterintelligence in Occupied Persia (Iran)* (London: Palgrave, 2015)

O'Sullivan, A., *German Covert Initiatives and British Intelligence in Persia (Iran) 1939–45* (Pretoria: University of South Africa, June 2012)

Öztürk, O.M., *Iki Dünya savasi arasindaki dönemde (1919–1939) stratejik acidan Türkiye* (Besinci Askeri Tarih Semineri Bildirileri, Ankara Genelkurmay Basim Evi, 1996)

Papen, F. von, *Memoirs* (Translated by Brian Connell) (London: Andre Deutsch, 1952)

Palmer, A., *The Gardeners of Salonika* (London: Andre Deutsch, 1965)

Pavlowitch, S., *Hitler's New Disorder* (London: Hurst, 2020)

Pavlowitch, S., *A History of the Balkans 1804–1945* (London: Longman, 1999)

Peakman, J., *Hitler's Island War* (London: I.B.Tauris, 2018)

Philliou, C., *Turkey: A Past Against History* (University of California Press, 2021)

Phillips, E., *Hitler's Last Hope* (W.H. Allen, 1942)

Pitt, B., *Wavell's Command* (London: Jonathan Cape, 1980)

Plowman, J., *Greece 1941: The Death Throes of Blitzkrieg* (Yorkshire: Pen & Sword, 2018)

Provence, Michael, *The Last Ottoman Generation* (Cambridge, 2017)

Pruskin, A., *Serbia Under the Swastika* (Illinois, 2017)

Rankin, N., *Churchill's Wizards* (London: Faber, 2008)

Rawson, A., *Balkan Struggles* (Yorkshire: Pen & Sword, 2020)

Roberts, G., 'Moscow's Cold War on the Periphery: Soviet Policy in Greece, Iran and Turkey, 1943–8', *Journal of Contemporary History*, Vol.46, No.1, pp.58–81

Rogers, A., *Churchill's Folly: Leros and the Aegean* (London: Cassell, 2003)

Rundt, S., 'The Army of the Crescent and the Star', *Infantry Journal*, February 1947, pp.18–23

Schofield, V., *Wavell: Soldier and Statesman* (London: John Murray, 2006)

Seligman, M., *No Stars to Guide* (Stroud, Gloucestershire: Sutton, 1997)

Sarafis, S, *ELAS: Greek Resistance Army* (London: Merlin Press, 1980)

Schevill, F., *A History of the Balkans* (New York: Dorset Press edition, 1991)

Schreiber, G. (ed.), *Germany and the Second World War: Volume 3: The Mediterranean, South-East Europe and North Africa 1939–1941* (London: Clarendon Press, 1995)

Seydi, S., 'The Activities of Special Operations Executive in Turkey', *Middle Eastern Studies*, 40:4, pp.153–170

Shaw, S. and Shaw, E.K., *History of the Ottoman Empire and Modern turkey Vol. II* (Cambridge University Press, 1977)

Shaw, S., *Turkey and the Holocaust* (London: Palgrave, 1993)

Shirer,W., *The Rise and Fall of the Third Reich* (New York: Simon & Schuster, 1960)

Shores, C., *Air War for Yugoslavia, Greece and Crete 1940–41* (London: Grub Street, 1987)

Simmons, M., *Agent Cicero* (Yorkshire: Spellmount, 2014)

Sivis, E., *The Raid on the Editorial Office of the Turkish Newspaper Office Tan, 1945*, RUDN, 2020 Vol.19 No.1, pp.197–213

Smiley, David, *Albanian Assignment* (London: Hogarth Press, 1984)

Smith, G., *Duty and Destiny: The Life and Faith of Winston Churchill* (Cambridge UP, 2020)

Smith, P., *War in the Aegean* (Mechanicsburg, PA: Stackpole, 2008)

Soyupak, Kemal, *Organisation and Duties of the Turkish Armed Forces* (Encyclopaedia of Republican Türkiye, İletişim Publishers)

Stankova, M., *Bulgaria in British Foreign Policy 1943–49* (LSE Thesis, 1999)

Tamkin, N., *Britain, Turkey and the Soviet Union, 1940–45* (London: Palgrave, 2009)

Tamkoc, M., *The Warrior Diplomats* (Utah, 1976)

Tarnstrom, R., *Balkan Battles* (Lindsborg, Kansas: Trogen Books, 1998)

Ter-Matevosyan, V., *Turkey, Kemalism and the Soviet Union* (London: Palgrave, 2019)

Thomas, N., *Axis forces in Yugoslavia 1941–5* (Oxford: Osprey, 1995)

Thomas, N., *Yugoslav Armies 1941–45* (Oxford: Osprey, 2022)

Todman, D., *Britain's War: A New World, 1942–1947* (Oxford UP, 2020)

Travlos, K. (ed,), *Salvation and Catastrophe* (Washington DC: Lexington Books, 2020)

Trigg, J., *Hitler's Jihadis* (Yorkshire: Spellmount, 2012)

Trifković, G., *Sea of Blood* (Warwick, Helion, 2022)

Tuncay, M., *The Turkish Army in the first years of the Second World War 1939–41* (Tarih ve Toplum, Nov 1986)

Turbett, C., *The Anglo-Soviet Alliance* (Yorkshire: Pen and Sword, 2021)

Ullrich, V., *Hitler, Downfall 1939–45* (Rochester, Kent: Vintage Digital, 2020)

Ungor, U., *Young Turk social engineering: mass violence and the nation state in eastern Turkey 1913–50* (University of Amsterdam, 2009)

Vali, F., *Bridge across the Bosporus* (John Hopkins University Press, 1971)

VanderLippe, J., *The Politics of Turkish Democracy* (State University of New York Press, 2005)

Wakefield, A., *Under the Devil's Eye* (Stroud, Gloucestershire: Sutton, 2004)

Warner, P., *Auchinleck: The Lonely Soldier* (Yorkshire: Pen & Sword, 2006)

Weber, F., *The Evasive Neutral* (Missouri Press, 1979)

Weisband, E., *Turkish Foreign Policy, 1943–45* (Princeton, 1973)

Williams, M., *Mussolini's Secret War in the Mediterranean and the Middle East: Italian Intelligence and the British Response* (Intelligence and National Security, 22:6, pp.881–904,)

Willingham, M., *Perilous Commitments – Battle for Greece and Crete 1940–41* (Yorkshire: Spellmount, 2005)

Woodbine-Parish, M., *Aegean Adventures 1940–43* (London: Book Guild, 1993)

Woodward, E., *Documents on British Foreign Policy – Third series* (Foreign Office, London, 1947)

Wylie, N., *European Neutrals and Non-Belligerents during the Second World War* (Cambridge, 2010)

Zurcher, E., *Turkey: A Modern History* (London: I.B.Tauris, 1992)

# NOTES

### Introduction
1. The case is made by Ferdinand Schevill in his classic *The History of the Balkan Peninsula* (Ayer Publishing, 1922).
2. C. Catherwood, *The Balkans in World War Two*, (Palgrave, 2003), p.169.
3. E. Weisband, *Turkish Foreign Policy, 1943–45*, (Princeton, 1973).
4. A.J.P. Taylor, *English History, 1914–1945* (Oxford, 1965), p.522.
5. G. Smith, *Duty and Destiny: The Life and Faith of Winston Churchill* (Cambridge UP, 2020).
6. R. Denniston, *Churchill's Secret War: Diplomatic Decrypts, the Foreign Office and Turkey, 1942–44* (History Press, 2009, Kindle e-book), Location 353.
7. Anon, *Turkish Officers – WWII memories* (Ankara: General Staff Military History and Strategic Studies Department, 1999).
8. S. Deringil, *Turkish Foreign Policy during the Second World War* (Cambridge, 1989).

### Chapter 1
1. For the causes and conduct of the war see, K. Travlos (Ed), *Salvation and Catastrophe* (Lexington Books, 2020). For a military history see, Edward J. Erikson, *The Turkish War of Independence* (Praeger, 2021).
2. M. Troulis, 'Kemalism on the March', in K. Travlos (Ed), *Salvation and Catastrophe* (Lexington Books, 2020). p.285.
3. P. Kinross, *Atatürk: The Rebirth of a Nation* (W&N, 2001), p.460.
4. C. King, *Midnight at the Pera Palace* (Norton, 2015).
5. J. McHugo, *Syria: A Recent History* (Saqi Books, 2015), Chapter 2.
6. In 2011, the Turkish Prime Minister apologised for the killing of 13,000 Kurds in the rebellion.
7. M. Heper, *The State and Kurds in Turkey* (Palgrave, 2007), p.141.
8. U. Ungor, *Young Turk social engineering: mass violence and the nation state in eastern Turkey 1913–50* (University of Amsterdam 2009).
9. J. Bulloch, *No Friends but the Mountains*, (Viking, 1992), p.90.
10. Heper, *The State and Kurds in Turkey*, Chapter 5.
11. C. Philliou, *Turkey: A Past Against History* (University of California Press, 2021).
12. J. VanderLippe, *The Politics of Turkish Democracy* (State University of New York Press, 2005), p7.
13. The National Archives (TNA) FO 371/E6800/135/44: Ambassador Loraine to Lord Halifax.
14. Denniston, *Churchill's Secret War*, Location 1027.
15. F. Weber, *The Evasive Neutral* (Missouri Press, 1979), p.24.
16. S. Shaw, *Turkey and the Holocaust*, (Palgrave, 1993), pp.14–15.
17. D. Barlas, 'Friends or Foes? Diplomatic Relations between Italy and Turkey, 1923–36', *International Journal of Middle East Studies* (May 2004), Vol. 36, No. 2, pp.231–252.
18. S. McMeekin, *The Berlin-Baghdad Express* (Allan Lane, 2010), pp.340–365.

### Chapter 2
1. A. Gould, *Special Duties*, (Sampson Low, 1945), p.41.
2. J. Hammerton, *The War Illustrated*, No.9, 11 November 1939.
3. Turkey: Law No. 1111 of 1927, Military Law (UNHCR, Refworld), https://www.refworld.org/docid/3ae6b4d020.html.
4. J. VanderLippe, 'The Politics of Turkish Democracy', p.47.
5. British notes say Mark IV but other sources say Mark VI, which seems more likely as Mark IV was used as a training tank.
6. British notes say BA27 but R. Tarnstrom (Balkan Battles) says BA6 and there are pictures to support this.
7. D. Barno, & N. Bensahel, *Adaptation Under Fire: How Militaries Change in Wartime* (Oxford, 2020).
8. TNA, *Notes on the Turkish Army 1940*, War Office.
9. S. Rundt, *The Army of the Crescent and the Star* (Infantry Journal), February 1947.
10. D. Akyüz, 'Legacy of the Stormtroop', in K. Travlos (Ed), *Salvation and Catastrophe* (Lexington Books, 2020), p.203.
11. Akyüz, *Legacy of the Stormtroop*, p.219.
12. VanderLippe, *The Politics of Turkish Democracy*, p.40.
13. Kinross, *Atatürk: The Rebirth of a Nation*, p.487.
14. The historian Erhan Çifci has highlighted the views of several officers graduating during the Second World War. https://twitter.com/dunyaharptarihi/status/1505257038112337920.
15. G. Leiser, 'The Turkish Air Force 1939–45', *Middle Eastern Studies*, Vol.26, No.3.
16. A. Gould, *Special Duties*, (Sampson Low, 1945), p.34.
17. TNA: FO371/E2214/44, Foreign Office Annual Report 1937.
18. D. Barlas, D, 'Friends or Foes? Diplomatic Relations between Italy and Turkey, 1923–36', *International Journal of Middle East Studies*, Vol. 36, No. 2, (May 2004) p.241.
19. S. Guvenc, *Building a Republican Navy in Turkey: 1924–1939* (International Journal of Naval History, Volume 1 Number 1, April 2002), p.10.

### Chapter 3
1. Known as the *Kalfoff-Politis Protocol*, September 1924.
2. D. Kousoulas, *The Price of Freedom: Greece in World Affairs 1939–53* (Pickle, 2016).
3. M. Stankova, *Bulgaria in British Foreign Policy 1943–49* (LSE Thesis, 1999), p.28.
4. N. Tamkin, N, *Britain, Turkey and the Soviet Union, 1940–45* (Palgrave, 2009).
5. Weber, 'The Evasive Neutral', p.52.
6. Barlas, 'Friends or Foes? Diplomatic Relations between Italy and Turkey, 1923–36', p.246.
7. L. Fischer, *The Soviets in World Affairs* (Princeton, 1951).
8. O. Isci, The Massigli Affair and its Context, *Journal of Contemporary History* (2020).
9. O. Isci, 'The Massigli Affair', p.10–11.
10. O. Isci, 'The Massigli Affair', p.14.
11. N. Sadak, 'Turkey Faces the Soviets', *Foreign Affairs* Vol. 27, No.3 (April 1949).
12. M.A. Hasretyan, *Turkiye'de Kurt Sorunu 1918–1940* (Instituya Kurdi, Berlin, 1995).
13. For an overview of the post-Ottoman Middle East see, Provence, M, *The Last Ottoman Generation* (Cambridge, 2017).
14. N. Gurboga, *Mine Workers, The State and War* (Bogazici University, 2005).

### Chapter 4
1. G. Clemenceau, French Deputy, Chamber of Deputies debate (June 1916).
2. TNA, FO 371/29782 Angora 670 28.3.41.

3   W. Churchill, *The World Crisis 1916–18* (Thornton Butterworth, 1927).
4   N. Milton, *Neville Chamberlain's Legacy* (Pen and Sword, 2019), p.163.
5   TNA, Prime Minister Aide Memoire: Balkan strategy.
6   E. Barker, *British Policy in South-East Europe*, (MacMillan, 1976), p.12.
7   TNA, CAB 65-2-29.
8   TNA, CAB 65-2-29, p.17.
9   TNA, CAB 84/7/13, JP (39 (13), Staff conversations with Greece.
10  TNA, CAB 80/2/8, Chiefs of Staff Committee: The Turkish Alliance.
11  TNA, WO 106/2065.
12  TNA, WO 106/2065.
13  TNA, WO 106/2065.
14  TNA, COS (39) 34: Halifax and the French Ambassador.
15  TNA, CAB 66/4/9, Memo, 18 September 1939: Gamelin to Ironside.
16  M. Cervi, *The Hollow Legions* (Doubleday, 1971), p.11.
17  E. May, *Strange Victory* (Hill and Wang, 2015), p.451.
18  TNA, CAB 65 W.M. 76 (40) 27.3-40.
19  Deringil, 'Turkish Foreign Policy during the Second World War', p.94.
20  Isci, 'The Massigli Affair and its Context', pp.1–26.
21  Catherwood, 'The Balkans in World War Two', p.75.
22  *Ibid*. p.90.

**Chapter 5**
1   Weber, 'The Evasive Neutral', p.52.
2   Deringil, 'Turkish Foreign Policy during the Second World War', p.101.
3   Isci, 'The Massigli Affair and its Context', pp.271–296.
4   Cervi, 'The Hollow Legions', p79.
5   J. Carr, *The Defence and Fall of Greece 1940–41*, (Pen & Sword, 2013).
6   For ORBATs, C. Shores, *Air War for Yugoslavia, Greece and Crete 1940–41* (Grubb Street, 1987), p.23.
7   Deringil, 'Turkish Foreign Policy during the Second World War', p.111.
8   *Ibid*. p.112.
9   K. Matev, *The Armoured Forces of the Bulgarian Army 1936–45* (Helion, 2015), p.43.
10  K. Matev, *Red Wind Over the Balkans* (Helion, 2019), p.65 for a table of equipment supplied.
11  M. Creveld, *Hitler's Strategy 1940–41 – The Balkan Clue* (Cambridge, 1973).
12  Creveld, 'Hitler's Strategy 1940–41 – The Balkan Clue', p.37.
13  W. Shirer, *The Rise and Fall of the Third Reich* (Simon & Schuster, 1960).
14  V. Ullrich, *Hitler, Downfall 1939–45* (Vintage Digital, 2020), p.139.
15  G. Blau, *Invasion Balkans* (Burd Street, 1997), p.14.
16  For the armed forces, Balkan Military History, <https://www.balkanhistory.org/royal-yugoslavian-armed-forces.html.>, accessed 16 August 2021.
17  N. Balfour, *Paul of Yugoslavia – Britain's Maligned Friend* (Hamish Hamilton, 1980), p.225.
18  A. Fort, *Wavell: Life and Times of an Imperial Servant* (Jonathan Cape, 2011), p.186.
19  J. Plowman, *Greece 1941 – The Death Throes of Blitzkrieg* (Pen & Sword, 2018), Chapter 11.
20  J. Hammerton, *The War Illustrated*, No.83, 4 April 1939.
21  TNA: WO190/983/22832, 79A, 6 February 1941.
22  V. O'Hara, V, *Struggle for the Middle Sea* (Naval Institute Press, 2009), p.XIV.
23  R. Belot, *The Struggle for the Mediterranean 1939–45* (Princeton, 1951), p.155.
24  D. Hobbs, *Taranto*, (Seaforth, 2020), p.20.
25  G. Gorodetsky, *Grand Delusion: Stalin and the German Invasion of Russia*, (New Haven, 1999).
26  G. Gorodetsky, 'Grand Delusion', p.247.
27  *Ibid*. p.156.
28  TNA: WO 201/73, Joint army/navy report of the operation & Colonel Symons 50 Commando.
29  TNA: WO 201/73, 9 March 1941.
30  W. Benyon-Tinker, *Dust upon the Sea* (Hodder & Stoughton, 1947).
31  J. Guard, *Improvise and Dare: War in the Aegean* (Book Guild, 1997).

**Chapter 6**
1   M. Tuncay, *The Turkish Army in the first years of the Second World War 1939–41* (Tarih ve Toplum, Nov 1986), p.41.
2   Deringil, 'Turkish Foreign Policy during the Second World War', p.122.
3   US Dept. of State, Holocaust files, <https://www.archives.gov/research/holocaust/finding-aid/civilian/rg-84-turkey.html>.
4   S. Kline, 'Unearthing WWII aircraft buried in Kayseri', <https://www.dailysabah.com/op-ed/2019/03/06/unearthing-wwii-aircraft-buried-in-kayseri>.
5   J. Barr, *A Line in the Sand*, (Simon and Shuster, 2011).
6   B. Pitt, *Wavell's Command* (Jonathan Cape, 1980), Location 5821.
7   B. James, *Hitler's Gulf War* (Pen & Sword 2009), p.207.
8   Deringil, 'Turkish Foreign Policy during the Second World War', p.95.
9   O'Hara, 'Struggle for the Middle Sea', p.133.
10  A. O'Sullivan, *Espionage and Counterintelligence in Occupied Persia* (Palgrave, 2015), p.252.
11  A. O'Sullivan, 'Espionage and Counterintelligence in Occupied Persia', p.128.
12  TNA: Ref. COS 116, C in C Middle East to War Office 7/9/41.
13  TNA: Ref COS (ME) 250, C in C Middle East to Air Ministry 17/4/41.
14  P. Alexiades, *Target Corinth Canal 1940-44* (Pen & Sword, 2015), Location 1792.
15  Weber, 'The Evasive Neutral', p.111.
16  VanderLippe, 'The Politics of Turkish Democracy', p.95.
17  Denniston, *Churchill's Secret War*, Location 1956.
18  Weber *The Evasive Neutra*', p.113.
19  Deringil, *Turkish Foreign Policy during the Second World War*, p.132.
20  M. Kerrigan, *WW2 Plans That Never Happened* (Amber Books, 2011).
21  R. Forczyk, *The Caucasus 1942–43: Kleist's Race for Oil* (Osprey, 2015).
22  Albert Speer, *Spandau: The Secret Diaries* (Macmillan, 1976), p.47.
23  Denniston, *Churchill's Secret War*, Location 1687.
24  E. Phillips, *Hitler's Last Hope* (W.H. Allen, 1942).
25  TNA: WO 201/1094.

**Chapter 7**
1   M. Howard, *The Mediterranean Strategy in the Second World War* (Greenhill, 1993).

2   See, W. Churchill, *The Turn of the Tide* (1957) and *The Triumph in the West* (1959).
3   R. Leighton, *Overlord Revisited*, (American Historical Review), July 1963.
4   S. Napier, *Churchill Military Genius or Menace?* (History Press, 2018) p.203.
5   A. Danchev & D. Todman, *War Diaries of Field Marshall Lord Alanbrooke* (W&N, 2001*)*, Location 10642.
6   M. Howard, *Grand Strategy Vol. IV* (HMSO, Kindle Edition).
7   Howard, *Grand Strategy*, Chapter XX.
8   N. Nicolson, *Alex* (Weidenfeld & Nicolson, 1973), p.71.
9   Howard, *Grand Strategy*, Chapter XX.
10  W. Churchill, *The Hinge of Fate: The Second World War, Volume 4* (Penguin, 2005).
11  Deringil, *Turkish Foreign Policy during the Second World War*, p.135.
12  E. Weisband, *Turkish Foreign Policy, 1943–45*, Chapter 6.
13  Denniston, *Churchill's Secret War*, Location 2457.
14  Leiser, *The Turkish Air Force 1939–45*, (Middle Eastern Studies, July 1990).
15  TNA: WO 201/1233.
16  TNA: WO 201/1233, Aid to Turkey 23 June 1943.
17  A. Avci, *Winning the war of perception: American attempts to counter Germany's military influence in Turkey during World War II*, (Turkish Studies, Nov. 2015).
18  Denniston, *Churchill's Secret War*.
19  M. Howard, *British Intelligence in the Second World War, Vol.5* (HMSO, 1990), p.ix–xi.
20  N. Rankin, *Churchill's Wizards*, (Faber 2009), pp.345–352.
21  TNA: WO 169/24911, Plan Barclay – Summary of radio messages, 14 July 1943.
22  TNA:, AIR 23/558, Barclay air action.
23  TNA: WO 169/249, Memo to Dudley Clarke 12 May 1943.
24  B. Macintyre, *Operation Mincemeat* (Bloomsbury, 2010).
25  D. Irving, D, *Trail of the Fox* (BCA edition, 1977) p.268.
26  Churchill, *The Second World War, Vol. 5*, p.161.
27  Weber, *The Evasive Neutral*, p.180.
28  Matev, *Red Wind over the Balkans*, p.69.
29  Matev, *Armoured Forces of the Bulgarian Army*, pp.113–114.
30  A. Mladenov, *The Bulgarian Air Force in the Second World War*, (Helion, 2018), p.41.
31  W. Benyon-Tinker, *Dust upon the Sea*, (Hodder & Stoughton, 1947).
32  Howard, *Grand Strategy Vol. IV*, Location 9025.
33  P. Smith, P, *War in the Aegean* (Stackpole, 2008), p.32.
34  B. O'Carroll, *The Long Range Desert Group in the Aegean* (Pen & Sword, 2020), gives a number of examples of Turkish cooperation.
35  TNA: Former Naval Person (Churchill) to President Roosevelt, 10 October 1943.
36  TNA: 9803A/7, Message Tedder to Eisenhower 6 October 1943.
37  TNA: WO 201/1675, Rhodes mission instructions 8 September 1943.
38  O'Hara, *Struggle for the Middle Sea*, p.229.
39  TNA: AIR 23/6222, Accolade Air Plan.
40  TNA: AIR 23/6222, Aegean Air Situation Reports describe the impact of German air superiority.
41  A. Rogers, *Churchill's Folly: Leros and the Aegean* (Cassell, 2003), p.235.
42  Churchill, *Closing the Ring*, p.195.
43  *Ibid*. p.408.
44  TNA: PM to General Ismay, 6 December 1943.
45  TNA: Middle East HQ to Eisenhower, 10 December 1943.
46  TNA: JPS memorandum No.37, 13 December 1943.
47  E. Packer, *Hard Lessons in the Aegean* (Purnell History of the Second World War), p.1516.
48  B. Lintott, *Anglo-Turkish Security and Intelligence, 1939–45*, (Routledge, 2018).
49  S. Seydi, *The Intelligence War in Turkey during WW2* (Middle East Studies) Vol.40, pp.75–85.
50  Denniston, *Churchill's Secret War*, Location 242.
51  E. Corse, *To accustom Turkish minds to a state of belligerency: The Delicate Balance of British Propaganda in Turkey during the Second World War*, (Journal of Balkan and Near Eastern Studies, Sept 2021). p.14.
52  O. Isci, O. *Anti-Soviet Activities in WW2 Turkey*, <http://crs.bilkent.edu.tr/from-our-archive/cicero/>.
53  Howard, *British Intelligence in the Second World War Vol.5*, p.50.
54  P. Leverkuehn, *German Military Intelligence* (Lucknow Books, 2016), p.70.
55  M. Simmons, *Agent Cicero* (Spellmount, 2014).
56  L. Moyzisch, L, *Operation Cicero* (Wingate, 1950).
57  A. O'Sullivan, *Nazi Secret Warfare in Occupied Persia (Iran)* (Palgrave 2014).
58  Gorodetsky, *Grand Delusion*, p.62.

**Chapter 8**

1   Tamkin, *Britain, Turkey and the Soviet Union, 1940–45*, p.141.
2   Weber, *The Evasive Neutral*, p.202.
3   Ullrich, *Hitler: The Downfall 1939–45*, p.396.
4   Hansard Fifth Series, Vol. 400, Column 1987.
5   Weisband, *Turkish Foreign Policy, 1943–45*, pp.266–268.
6   VanderLippe, *The Politics of Turkish Democracy*, p.99.
7   Hansard, HC Deb 02 August 1944 Vol. 402 at 1485.
8   TNA: CAB 80/75, 19 October 1943.
9   S. Kepher, *Cossac: Lt.Gen. Sir Frederick Morgan and the Genesis of Operation Overlord*, (Naval Institute Press, 2020), p.180.
10  Hamilton, N, *Monty, Master of the Battlefield 1942–44*, (Hamish Hamilton, 1983), p.457.
11  Howard, *British Intelligence in the Second World War Vol.5*, p.137.
12  TNA: WO 204/217, Plan Zeppelin.
13  TNA: Prem 3/447/8, 24 May 1944.
14  TNA: Air 20/4548, Plan Royal Flush, 11 May 1944.
15  For more on the purpose of deception operations, T.Holt, *The Deceivers: Allied Military Deception in the Second World War* (Lisa Drew Books, 2004).
16  TNA: COS(44) 415 (0), Memorandum of the First Sea Lord.
17  TNA: WO 201/1781, Memo from Middle East Command, April 1944.
18  S. Sarafis, *ELAS: Greek Resistance Army*, (Merlin Press, 1980), p.231.
19  J. Guard, *Improvise and Dare* (Book Guild, 1997).
20  Barker, *British Policy in South-East Europe*, p.117, argues that this figure is controversial.
21  F. Lindsay, *Beacons in the Night* (Stanford, 1993).
22  For the full story: G. Freeman, *The Forgotten 500* (NAL, 2007).
23  Lulushi, A, *Donavan's Devils* (Arcade 2016), location 1148.
24  T.E. Lawrence, *Arab Bulletin*, 20 August 1917, Article 15.
25  R. Bailey, *The Wildest Province*, (Jonathan Cape, 2008), p.38.
26  D. Brewer, *Greece, The Decade of War* (I.B.Tauris, 2016), p.138.
27  Barker, 'British Policy in South-East Europe', p.186.
28  TNA: Brigadier Clarke, Plan Zeppelin Amendment 5, 4 May 1944.
29  C. Catherwood, *Churchill and Tito* (Front-line, 2017), Chapter 4.
30  TNA: WO201/1582, Operation Knockholt.

31  See his memoirs, *Commando Crusade* (William Kimber, 1987).
32  For details of operations see; M. McConville, *A Small War in the Balkans* (Macmillan, 1986).
33  J. Dugan, *Ploesti* (Random House, 1982).
34  Mladenov, *The Bulgarian Air Force in the Second World War*, p.71.
35  Matev, *Red Wind over the Balkans*, p.134.
36  Hobbs, *Taranto*, p.381.
37  Tamkin, *Britain, Turkey and the Soviet Union, 1940–45*, p.159.
38  TNA: WO 219/981, Memo from Alexander to SHAEF, March 1945.
39  G. Roberts, *Moscow's Cold War on the Periphery: Soviet Policy in Greece, Iran and Turkey, 1943–8* (Journal of Contemporary History), Vol. 46, No. 1, p.59.

**Chapter 9**
1  Danchev & Todman, *War Diaries of Field Marshall Lord Alanbrooke*, location 9559.
2  Napier, *Churchill Military Genius or Menace*, p.362, highlights many of them.
3  TNA: British Ambassador at Ankara to Lord Halifax, June 30, 1942.

## ABOUT THE AUTHOR

Dave Watson lives in Scotland. He has been the editor of 'Balkan Military History' (www.balkanhistory.org) for over 23 years. He has contributed to a number of books, magazines and journals. Dave is a graduate in Scots Law from the University of Strathclyde and a Fellow of the Royal Society of Arts. He retired in 2018 as Head of Policy and Public Affairs at UNISON Scotland and now works part-time as a policy consultant. He is the secretary of Glasgow and District Wargaming Society – one of the UK's longest running wargame clubs. You can also follow Dave on Twitter @Balkan_Dave.